Rolling with the Press

Rolling with the Press
A PUBLISHER'S JOURNEY

By Edward Lehman
⋄ and ⋄
Suzanne Barrett

FILTER PRESS, LLC
Palmer Lake, Colorado

Rolling with the Press: A Publisher's Journey
ISBN: 978-0-86541-191-3
Library of Congress Control Number: 2016946793

©2016 by Edward Lehman. All rights reserved.

The original colored pencil drawings of the Longmont newspaper buildings used on the cover were drawn by the late Tom Currey, former art teacher at Longmont High School. The drawing of the *Longmont Daily Times-Call* building was done in 1988 by Jane Wikstrand, a student of Tom Currey.

BOOK & COVER DESIGN by Bookends Design, Boulder, Colorado

Printed in the United States of America

P.O. Box 95
Palmer Lake, CO 80133
888.570.2663
FilterPressBooks.com

This book is dedicated to the memory of my Grandfather, Edward Lehman Sr.

Contents

Acknowledgments — ix

PART 1: **The Early Years**
Chapter 1 – Gold Nugget on the Frontier Trail — 3
Chapter 2 – Thwarted Kidnapping — 15
Chapter 3 – Star Witness — 19

PART 2: **Youth and Childhood in Denver**
Chapter 4 – 920 Pennsylvania Street — 23
Chapter 5 – Another Kidnapping — 27
Chapter 6 – Evergreen — 33
Chapter 7 – Cuba — 41
Chapter 8 – Military School — 47

PART 3: **Roads Taken**
Chapter 9 – DU and the Rocky Mountain News Years — 53
Chapter 10 – Fires and Gambling — 57
Chapter 11 – Railroaded at Union Station — 63
Chapter 12 – Secret Service Agent's Service to Colorado — 69
Chapter 13 – Southern Colorado Bank Robberies — 73
Chapter 14 – A Couple of Fellas Named Roy — 79
Chapter 15 – The In-Between Years — 83
Chapter 16 – Ruth Gillespie — 85
Chapter 17 – Narrow Escape in Idaho Springs — 95
Chapter 18 – Years in Denver District Attorney Office — 97
Chapter 19 – The Doodlebug Case — 101
Chapter 20 – Colorado State Legislature — 105
Chapter 21 – Private Law Practice — 107

PART 4: **The Publishing Years**

Chapter 22 – Our Newspaper Publishing Adventure Begins   113
Chapter 23 – 1950s—On the Brink of Prosperity and Growth   123
Chapter 24 – Denver Real Estate   135
Chapter 25 – 1960s—A Time of Awakening   137
Chapter 26 – Expansion to the North—Loveland   147
Chapter 27 – 1970s—Growing into a New Generation   153
Chapter 28 – When the Rivers Roared!   161
Chapter 29 – Adjusting the Rudder and Steering Operations   175
Chapter 30 – Arsonist   181
Chapter 31 – Competition   183
Chapter 32 – Our Two-front War   189
Chapter 33 – Expansion to the South–Cañon City   193
Chapter 34 – A Building Sale—Maybe   207
Chapter 35 – 1980s—New Frontier of Each Dawning Day   209
Chapter 36 – A Century of Newspapering in Loveland   213
Chapter 37 – 1990s—Wars Without and Within   231
Chapter 38 – A Terrible Loss   239

PART 5: **The 21st Century**

Chapter 39 – The First Decade—2000-2010   243
Chapter 40 – Hold the Press!   255

Acknowledgments

The idea of writing this book has been on my mind for many years. The usual "too busy" excuses caused me to continue to think about it, never finding the time to gather all of the facts together until I retired at age 85. At that time, my wife, Connie, encouraged me to get started. She thought it would be a wonderful gift for me to give to my family.

Once I was underway, I reached out to my friend and associate, Izorah Suzanne Barrett to work with me. I sincerely thank her for her dedication and amazing talent with the research she did over the four years we worked on the book together. Suzanne not only researched and gathered all of the information and photos, but through her twice a week interviews, helped me to enjoy and remember the wonderful experiences and exciting times I have been given as a reporter, attorney, public servant, and newspaper publisher. I am forever grateful for her determination and kindhearted spirit.

We also worked closely with Doris and Tom Baker at Filter Press. We extend our heartfelt appreciation to them for their guidance, outstanding editing suggestions, photo enhancements, and kindness to us during this project.

At the completion of the book, we invited my son and editor Dean Lehman in to check our facts and do the final editing. We thank him for his skills and suggestions. He said we did a good job, and we hope you will think the same and enjoy the book.

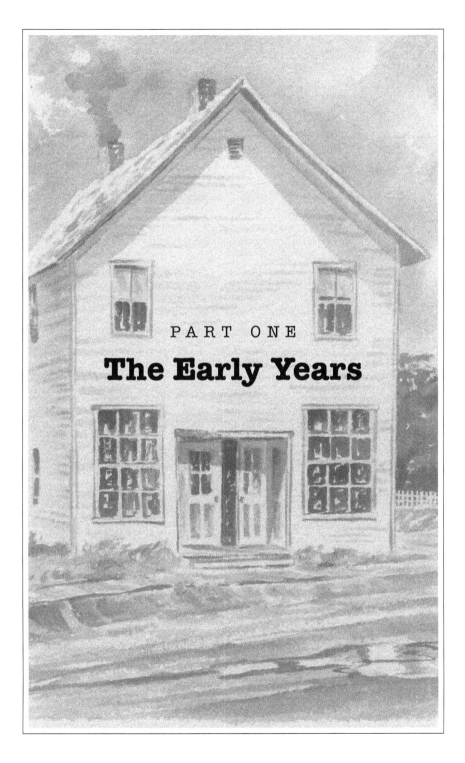

PART ONE

The Early Years

My great-grandfather, Nicholas Lehman, seventh from the right, in front of the Nicholas Lehman Boot & Shoe Company in the 1870s.

Chapter One

GOLD NUGGET ON THE FRONTIER TRAIL

IT IS NOT SURPRISING THE AMERICAN WEST has captured the imagination of the world. Against the beauty and grandeur of the vast plains and mountains, the struggle for existence creates a grand spectacle. Since it opened up more than a century ago, the West has excited the imagination.

The Wild West had heroes who became legends, but it was largely inhabited and settled by ordinary men and women who accomplished extraordinary things, often with little more than an idea, their bare hands, and a shovel. From the business entrepreneurs, clerks, doctors, farmers and ranchers, homemakers, innkeepers, and lawyers to the ministers and missionaries, merchants, Indian tribes, peddlers, publishers, and teachers—thousands of peaceful people were responsible for settling the West.

My grandfather was one of them. Edward Lehman Sr. devoted much of his life to a wholesale jewelry business in Denver. At seventeen, he had his first job as an outside salesman for his father, Nicholas Lehmann, who was born in Bavaria in 1834. After coming to America, he established the Nicholas Lehmann Boot & Shoe Company in Buffalo, New York. Because of strong feelings against Germans in 1874, the family eventually dropped an n from Lehmann to Americanize the name.

Grandfather's mother, the former Caroline Lingseiler, was also a native of Germany. She was brought to this country by her parents in the latter part of the 1830s. She eventually moved to New York City where she died at the age of 84, after rearing twelve children. Four of the sons—Edward and Lewis of Colorado, John of Buffalo, and Henry of Kansas—were still living in the 1870s. John continued his father's pioneer boot and shoe manufacturing business and his son, Charles, opened a freight hauling business.

Grandfather's nephew, Charles Lehman, went into the freight hauling business. His warehouse was located in Buffalo, New York. This photo was taken during the Civil War era, and it has long drawn conjecture among family members as to whether the wagons were actually loaded with apples (as indicated on the back of the photo) or if they were loaded with muskets and rifles for use by Union forces.

During the Civil War, Nicholas Lehman, along with his oldest son, Lewis, and youngest son, William, enlisted in the Union Army. Lewis enlisted in Erie County, New York, in September 1863, as a private in Captain Samuel Mahon's Company "L", 12th Regiment New York Volunteer Cavalry, under Colonel James W. Savage. He served three years, participating in many engagements and battles. The regiment had lost 427 soldiers—killed, wounded, or missing—by the end of the war. Lewis was wounded at Snow Hill, N.C., in March 1865, by gunshot in the upper left thigh and was honorably discharged in June.

William also saw combat, but his father, who served in Wiedrich's Battery of the 65th New York Volunteers, was mustered out at Harrisburg before seeing active service.

It isn't known or has been forgotten where Lewis settled after the war, but he lived out his last years at Fitzsimmons Army Hospital in Denver because of consumption, now known as tuberculosis, and because he had lost his eyesight. My memory of Uncle Lewis is scant, but I do recall occasional weekends when Grandfather, Mother, and I drove to see him at the hospital. He would pat my head saying, "Yes, this is a fine young boy, and I'm sorry I can't see him." He is buried in the soldier's field at Fairmount Cemetery.

Grandfather, the third eldest son of Nicholas and Caroline, was born in 1857. He became ill with pneumonia and was in declining health.

Grandfather as a young boy, age 8 or 9, in Buffalo, New York.

Doctors advised him that if he wanted to live, he must get out of the damp climate of Buffalo and go west where the air was much better and, if possible, get an outdoor job.

With virtually no funds, he set his sights westward and arrived in Colorado in September 1879. In Colorado's high and dry climate, he regained his strength sufficiently to get work on a ranch in the Castle Rock area. He and a faithful dog herded a large flock of sheep and kept them safe from predators day and night. The curative powers of the clean air apparently worked very well because in a matter of months his health was fully restored.

However, Grandfather's natural talents lay more in sales than in herding sheep so he traveled to Denver where he was fortunate to get a job with C. W. Little, then the only wholesale jeweler in the city. He spent most of his time as a traveling salesman representing the company to jewelry stores in Denver and north all the way to the Canadian border.

In those early years, a system of stagecoaches linked the mining communities and small towns of the West. Grandfather said he always rode on the top deck with the driver of the team because he wanted to be prepared to jump at a moment's notice in case the stage got too close to a precipitous fall of several hundred feet.

Grandfather kept a lot of jewelry stores in business. In the 1880s, mining was the predominant industry in Colorado. Grandfather supplied the jewelers who sold to the miners, who were big buyers of jewelry. Many had girlfriends and some had distant brides as well, but they didn't bring them West in every instance so they were eager to buy jewelry to send to them.

Grandfather called on many types of stores, gaining knowledge of the jewelry business. A biographer, Wilbur Fiske Stone, noted in volume IV of his *History of Colorado* that Grandfather was a student of progressive thinking by studying what needed to be done to develop and improve the business.

In 1882 he formed his own wholesale jewelry business, and in 1885, began a partnership with C. M. Blythe under the name Blythe & Lehman at the corner of 16th and Blake Streets, in the Witter block of Denver.

In March 1885 Grandfather married Pauline A. Fischer, a native of Portsmith, Ohio. She too had consumption, and her doctors in Ohio had urged her to go west to breathe the rare air and enjoy the outdoor climate of Colorado. As did Grandfather's, her health made a dramatic improvement.

Grandfather as a young man in early-day Colorado, at about age 25, when he opened his first jewelry business in Denver.

Edward and Pauline Fischer Lehman enjoying one of their frequent excursions to the mountains west of Denver.

Most homes in Denver at this time had screened outdoor porches where people lived and spent the night hours during the summer months. After marrying, Edward and Pauline searched Denver for an apartment and after many disappointments were pleased to find one painted completely white, but there was a problem. The previous family of four who lived in the apartment had all died from diphtheria, so the hunt resumed for a place to live. When Grandfather wrote to his father to give him the great word about his marriage, his father wrote back saying that he was happy to hear that Grandfather no longer needed his help. While this was not quite the case, Grandfather and his new bride watched every penny, eventually reaching a point of great comfort. They had one daughter, Anna Amelia, born in 1886.

Denver was growing but it was still a rugged cattleman's town at the edge of the plains on the Western frontier. Mother often recalled as a small child seeing the Indian teepees along Cherry Creek with the women cooking and moving about in camp while the men rode to and fro on horseback. Wagon train encampments were circled on the outskirts of town

My mother, Anna, age 8 or 9.

where the occupants stopped to replenish their supplies and rest before continuing their journey westward.

Although Grandfather's jewelry business was small in scale to start, it quickly built a steady clientele, and by 1887, the firm of Blythe, Lehman & Company was well established and they took on another partner, C. H. Green. However, after only one year this partnership was dissolved and Grandfather moved on to set up another jewelry business of his own.

By 1893 he had admitted a partner, W. W. Hamilton, under the name Lehman & Hamilton, which remained in business until 1902, when that partnership too was dissolved with each party creating independent businesses.

There were challenges such as during the silver panic of 1893. Business dropped drastically and Grandfather was forced to close the jewelry store and pull in all of the salesmen from the road. Within a matter of a few weeks, he was able to reopen the store.

In 1894, as Grandfather was getting back on his feet, one of his older brothers, Frederick, came west to Colorado because he had contracted tuberculosis in the heavily polluted air from the steel mills in and around Buffalo. He arrived with his wife and their four young children. They homesteaded in Aurora. Grandfather loaned them money for the purchase of property at the corner of Colorado Boulevard and Florida Avenue. They

A renowned beauty, Anna Amelia Lehman grew up in Denver.

Edward Lehman Sr.

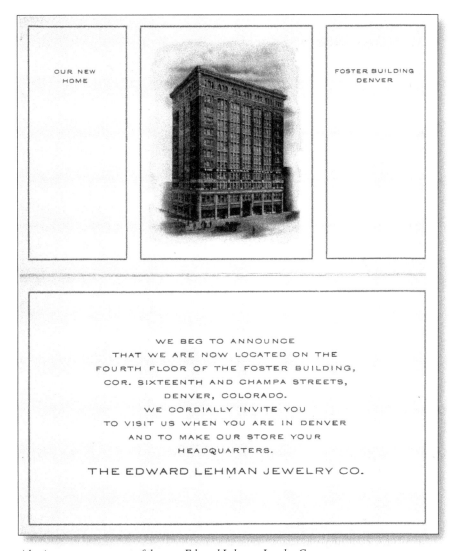

A business announcement of the new Edward Lehman Jewelry Company

built a greenhouse and began growing vegetables, but soon changed their product line to carnations because there was a better market for flowers. However, after only two years in Colorado, Frederick died.

The Edward Lehman Jewelry Company was incorporated in 1904 with Grandfather filling the roles of president and treasurer and his wife's sister, Bertha A. Fischer, as accountant and secretary. By now his business had extended its reach well beyond Colorado to include Wyoming, Utah, New Mexico, Montana, and Idaho.

Grandfather moved his business to the newly constructed A. C. Foster building at 16th and Champa Streets. The movers brought his safes upstairs through the elevator shaft where he eventually had two complete floors for showrooms and watch repairs. The business grew to support a staff of fifteen, including road sales representatives and watchmakers. He had a steady stream of railroad people who came in to get their timepieces checked. They relied heavily on their watches to conduct timely communications and to keep the trains moving on schedule.

It was a good-looking jewelry store and became a complete pillar of jewelry stores located in what would later be known as the University Building. The company published an annual catalog of fancy jewelry of all types. The store also offered silver services and other items cherished by homeowners of that era. Mother often looked back favorably upon

The Edward Lehman Jewelry Company showroom in the A. C. Foster Building with clocks, watches, silver services, and silverware displayed in glass cases. The jewelry company also maintained a sizeable watch repair department.

Large vaults lined the back wall of the company. Each night valuable items were placed in them for safekeeping.

Christmas Eves when the family visited the jewelry store and she chose jewelry and other fine items right up to the stroke of midnight.

Grandfather was a member and trustee of the 23rd Avenue Presbyterian Church for twenty-three years. He also was a member of the Denver Rotary Club, the Denver Civic and Commercial Association, and the Unity Camp, No. 25 of the Woodmen of the World. He belonged to the Union Lodge, No. 7 AF & AM; the Denver Chapter, No. 29 R. A. M.; the Colorado Commandery, No. 1, K. T.; Colorado Consistory, No. 1, S. P. R. S.; the Council, R. & S. M.; and to the Mystic Shrine. During World War I, he sold war bonds too and built up a splendid sales record.

Mother's first, and favorite, husband was Hector C. McNaught, a mining engineer from Denver, whom she married in 1912. She divorced Mr. McNaught in 1920 and later married Harry A. Stier, a jewelry salesman in Grandfather's company and my father. Within three months of my birth in 1925, he was no longer around, and Mother divorced him in 1929. She and Grandfather raised me, and in 1935, I took Grandfather's name. Mother's third and final husband, Henry J. Lucke, was a patent attorney in New York.

Chapter Two

THWARTED KIDNAPPING

PNEUMONIA WAS A DEADLY DISEASE IN THE EARLY 1900S, especially in Colorado's high altitude. Pneumonia combined with the flu took my Grandmother Pauline's life at the age of 60 in 1920. Fortunately, her sister, Bertha, stayed on with us as the chief accountant and resident manager of the jewelry store whenever Grandfather was out of town. Aunt Bertha was a dearly loved member of the family and her dedication to us and the company was steadfast and true. She worked in the company until 1929 when Grandfather sold the business to A. C. Becken, a national jewelry wholesale company out of Chicago.

Once retired, Grandfather began to look for warmer places to spend his winters. During one of his trips, he was seated on a bench in a large park in Los Angeles when he met a retired wholesale ready-to-wear women's clothier and struck up a daily acquaintance with him.

Denver had long been the summer headquarters of a gang of bunko artists who enjoyed the pleasant weather while looking for suckers to invest in, of all things, horseracing. Grandfather's new friend in Los Angeles, "Mr. Rainier," insisted that Grandfather place a bet on a sure thing in a horse race. Grandfather said he really didn't want to do that as he didn't understand anything about horseracing. "Mr. Rainier" and his partners assured him he should just stay calm while they placed a bet for him. To get him to place the bet, they needed to sell him a scheme and in turn, get their hands on any funds he had readily available. "Mr. Rainier" and his partners had likely followed Grandfather to Los Angeles from Denver where they had become aware he had sold his jewelry business.

HING—SUNDAY MORNING, MAY 20, 1934

HARGED WITH
ROLL ROBBERIES

Daughter Saves Father's Cash

FATHER SAVED FROM SWINDLE BY DAUGHTER

(Continued From Page One.)

weeks ago. Cramer represented himself as a representative of a western race horse syndicate.

Together they made a purported bet on a race. Lehman was told they had won $50,570, but they would have to show that if they had lost they would have been able to pay.

Lehman obtained drafts for $2,700 and $5,700, and rejoined the couple. Rainer pretended to put up $18,000 as his and Cramer's share. The trio then flew to Seattle on Rainer's claim that the women's ready-to-wear concern which he represented had transferred him to Aberdeen, Wash.

While awaiting approval of Lehman's drafts, the trio registered at a hotel in Tacoma.

In the meantime, Mrs. Lucke had ordered payment stopped on the drafts. She also notified a detective agency in Los Angeles whose representative, A. D. Marshall, former Denver policeman, asked Tacoma officers to arrest Lehman's "friends." The detention of Rainer followed, but Cramer had disappeared.

LEFT MONEY WITH CLERK AT HOTEL.

Arresting officers said Rainer had represented to Lehman that his $18,000 was contained in a roll of bills, which actually contained two $100 bills and seventy-eight $1 bills. Rainer had left the roll with the clerk of the hotel in Tacoma.

Lehman's home, where Mrs. Lucke's son, Lehman Lucke, 9, is staying with his aunt, was without details of the attempted swindle, altho it was said that Mrs. Lucke and Lehman were expected back from Los Angeles Tuesday or Wednesday.

Mrs. Lucke has been staying with her father since his injuries last July. Her husband is in New York.

The method tried on Lehman recently was used by Walter Elmer Mead, alias John H. Foster, "the Christ Kid," in mulcting Martin Wunderlich, St. Paul, Minn., and Jefferson City, Mo., contractor of $50,000, and resulted in revelation that Mead, a fugitive, had associated himself with Dillinger gangsters in Chicago. Mead used the same method in Denver in 1922 in attempting to fleece H. Rasmussen of Rawlins, Wyo., of $25,000. He served a prison term in the Colorado prison at Canon City for that attempt.

Great Britain leads other countries in sending tourists to France last year, with the United States second

MRS. HENRY J. LUCKE and EDWARD LEHMAN.
Sharpers' efforts to swindle Lehman of $8,400 were thwarted by his daughter's suspicions, and resulted in the arrest Saturday of a fleeing suspect in Tacoma, Wash. The father and daughter are expected back in Denver early this week.

At the time this story garnered a number of headlines in the Rocky Mountain News *and the* Denver Post. *Efforts to swindle Grandfather were thwarted by Mother's suspicions and resulted in the arrest of one of the suspects in Tacoma, Washington.*

Two things took place—one, they placed a sizeable bet on a horse and second, the horse did a marvelous job of winning the race! This changed everything. They were happy to tell Grandfather that he had just won a large amount of money. This was, of course, the beginning of an old-time con game.

However, things were not as simple as they sounded because Grandfather had to produce the actual cash to show that he could have covered a loss if it occurred. The gang insisted Grandfather accompany them to visit with their auditor in Hoquiam, Washington, a place chosen because it was a sleepy little town making it an ideal place where they could grab his money and run. Grandfather had never flown before, but they got him onto a plane and then he just disappeared from California. Grandfather was directed to send a large draft to the Denver U. S. National Bank for his entire account to be shipped in cash.

Meanwhile, Mother's concern for her father's safety was growing. So much so that she traveled to Los Angeles and began her own investigation. Once she uncovered the plot, she reported it to the local authorities and hired a private detective agency to trace Grandfather's whereabouts and locate the gang's so-called auditor as he awaited the bank draft to clear the Denver U. S. National Bank. Mother stopped payment on the draft and the bank agreed because they realized something untoward was happening.

Mother, armed with information from the private detective and the bank on where to send the draft, phoned Grandfather in Hoquiam and told him that his newfound "friends" were confidence men and crooks. Eventually, the bunko men were arrested and made to post nominal bonds, which they immediately ignored by skipping town.

Grandfather arranged to get back to Denver by train where he was the subject of much newspaper publicity claiming he and his daughter had foiled a kidnapping and bunko plot. *The Denver Post*, in a weekend edition of the Hall of Fame, listed Mother as the savior of her father and she was praised by many for doing a fine job of police work in California. As for Grandfather, he soon began vacationing in places other than Los Angeles.

With his knowledge of jewelry stores, Grandfather could always find ready buyers for the rare stones he kept in velvet covered jewel cases. He would hide the jewel cases under his pillow when he traveled. One day he forgot one, and a hotel housekeeper turned it in to her boss. The wire services picked up the story and publicized it nationwide. Although Grandfather continued to travel, he no longer carried jewels, being aware of the threat and tragedy that followed jewelry salesmen. However, all the unsolicited publicity, from Grandfather's brush with the kidnapping and con artists to the return of his jewel case, was now causing great alarm and anxiety within the family for my safety as well.

Chapter Three

STAR WITNESS

AT SOME POINT MOTHER WAS INTRODUCED by a long-time family acquaintance to a man named Homer Ashley, who was promoting a dry cleaning machine that he said would revolutionize the dry cleaning industry. He claimed to hold the patents on the machine. Mother advanced him several thousand dollars to construct a model as she thought it sounded promising.

He even went so far as to name the manufacturing company Edward Lehman Enterprises in honor of Grandfather, which Mother later tried to prevent him from using. She was made president of the company but had no authority or duties.

Mother held the view that once in the business she had to protect her initial investment. While she did recoup some of her money, she never recovered all that she had given to Ashley or any of the money she spent covering bills she had guaranteed.

Never one to be a victim for long, especially when she became aware of the facts, after learning more about Ashley and consulting an attorney, Mother severed all connections with him. Soon she was cooperating with the Security and Exchange Commission to make sure Ashley was arrested. She became a star witness in the federal case after working quietly for more than a year with federal investigators, providing the needed links in their case against him.

Ashley's various operations netted him more than $100,000 in just a few years. He and his partner, Ernest Hetzel, were eventually convicted on twelve of the fifteen counts of using the mails to defraud. One count was dismissed, and they were found not guilty on two counts relating to a violation of the Securities Act.

Mother and Duggan

PART TWO
Youth and Childhood In Denver

The Lehman home at 920 Pennsylvania Street.

Chapter Four

920 PENNSYLVANIA STREET

OUR HOME, LOCATED IN THE CAPITOL HILL AREA OF DENVER, had a deep cement-covered driveway, which became quite icy and treacherous during the winter. Our household consisted of my Mother, Anna, Grandfather—never without his pipe—and Grandfather's sister-in-law, Aunt Bertha Fischer. Grandfather and Aunt Bertha retired after the sale of his business in 1929 when I was four.

Also living in the house were Maggie and Dick Buchanan, who were our housekeeper and handyman. Some of my earliest memories are of talking to them as a very young child. I had a nursemaid, Edith Huffacher, and there was a cook, Mrs. Sage, who was always anxious to get through the supper dishes so she could hurry home.

Our household always included a family dog. In Grandfather's younger days, he had a bulldog named Buddy. We also had a bulldog named General Pershing, but my great pal and favorite was Duggan (pronounced Doo-gan), an aggressive Boston bulldog. Added to this motley crew was Mike, a very independent gray Angora cat. Mike had a number of friends in a neighborhood gang. Once we arrived home worried about poor Mike just in time to see him the center of attention in a group of neighborhood cats. As he sent a right and then a left to another cat's jaw, they all adjourned.

Mike was our stalwart, and he was fairly obedient to Grandfather. He completed the list of retired seniors and when he wanted to come in, it usually was not long before dawn. He had a sad growl he produced as he marched around the house. Sometimes he would sit for hours on top of the brick ash pit (trash incinerator) contemplating his next bird snacks. Mother would send me out to pick him up and retire him for the evening.

The author in 1931 at Dora Moore Elementary School.

As a young boy I published my own newspaper, *The Evening Star*, covering neighborhood events of the day. Didn't everybody? I now question some of the content. It was mostly about the activities of our dogs and cats and things like that.

Next door to us on the south was a great old mansion finished in white with the windows of the parlor room highlighted with blue reflective lights. To the north was the Grant home with its principal occupant, Dr. Grant, a retired southern army surgeon.

Across the street were the Lippe brothers who had a great home on the corner. They lived with their invalid sister, who may have had Alzheimer's and was always accompanied by a white-uniformed nurse. At one point Mother decided to be social and we called on them. The invalid sister was unable to eat and her conversation was limited to about three cordial words somewhat strung together.

The Lippe brothers started each day by heading off in their chauffeur driven sedan to their downtown brokerage firm, where they could get the latest developments on the stock market.

When I was eight my two best pals were my cat, Mike, and my Boston bulldog, Duggan.

A little farther up the block, the Pierson house was home to a Colorado Fuel & Iron executive and at the corner was a home that housed a tough bulldog. Finally, an apartment house built on the opposite corner was home to a semi-retired couple who had been in the floral business.

Immediately in back of us was the Buchtel family. Henry A. Buchtel was a former Colorado governor (1907–1909) and had been chancellor at the University of Denver from 1899 to 1920. We also had a neighbor named Mr. Evans, an optometrist who often backed his car out into our ash pit, which did not make for a good relationship with Mother.

Mike enjoyed stepping next door to add full flavor to Dr. Grant's mint leaves growing in his garden. This made Dr. Grant very mad because he loved the mint juleps he made with the mint. In the evenings, when the house quieted down, Mike would begin his sepulchral march about the house to see if he could come in for the night, having declared hunting closed.

I had a Lionel electric train that had lighted windows. I welcomed the opportunity to show Mike how it looked approaching the station even though he was traveling with a "don't cross me" look on his face.

Once, we left Mike in the car to guard a mink stole belonging to one of Mother's friends. He proceeded to eat the stole, head and all. (In those days some furs had the stuffed heads of the animals attached.) He must have thought it was another cat trespassing on his territory.

Chapter Five

ANOTHER KIDNAPPING

MOTHER, ALWAYS BUSY DEVELOPING HER REAL ESTATE CAREER and frequently out of town, often left me alone with Aunt Bertha in the Pennsylvania house. It was a great old place with seventeen rooms, and it creaked a lot at night. Aunt Bertha and I could hear doors open and close on the floors below. On reflection, the house was something of a fortress because once we had locked all of the doors in the upstairs hall, it was well secured.

To further our security we acquired the services of a retired World War I infantry captain, Mr. Walters, who slept in the sewing room on the second floor. He came with his service revolver, a .45-caliber handgun, and was on duty at night.

The second floor had approximately ten doors off the hall, all going into bedrooms. Not all were occupied, but we had to lock everything up at night. The old house provided its own series of footfalls, creaks and groans, which Aunt Bertha and I had gotten used to, but we were still aware of the considerable threat from burglars, kidnappers, and prowlers. That is why we had Captain Walters and his handy automatic. The daytime people all carried their own guns too.

This was all playing out in my young world against a backdrop of the Roaring Twenties. Soon Prohibition would begin and end and then everything would come crashing down sending America into the Great Depression, lasting well into the mid-1930s.

A rather famous kidnapping took place on January 1, 1933, just two blocks from our house. Mr. Charles Boettcher II, a wealthy Denver businessman, was kidnapped at gunpoint from the driveway of his home. He was the grandson and namesake of one of Colorado's most prominent residents, Charles Boettcher, who started out by opening hardware stores in Greeley, Fort Collins, and Boulder in the 1870s. By the early 1900s, he had organized Great Western Sugar Company and the Portland (Ideal) Cement Company and was president of Denver and Salt Lake Railroad. In 1917 he built a summer home and hunting lodge on Lookout Mountain and in 1922 became joint owner of the Brown Palace Hotel in downtown Denver.

The name Boettcher has been associated with many prominent organizations such as the Boettcher Foundation and the Boettcher Scholarship program and distinctive civic buildings like the Boettcher Concert Hall and the Boettcher Mansion, now the state's Governor's Mansion.

Ultimately, Charles Boettcher II was released after $60,000 in ransom was paid by his family. The man behind the kidnapping, Verne Sankey, was caught some time later while sitting in a barber's chair in Chicago getting a haircut. Sankey was one of the first criminals to be labeled "Public Enemy No. 1" by the FBI.

While Boettcher was missing, Aunt Bertha and I had daily telephone calls from the Associated Press and United Press International, as well as local news reporters from the *Denver Post* and the *Rocky Mountain News*, looking for updates on the case. I believe most of the neighbors were aware of the kidnapping of Mr. Boettcher as well as other threats from burglars and prowlers. Aunt Bertha and I did a good job of answering questions for the press and for the police as to what was going on.

We became quite close to several members of the Denver Police Department who were keeping an eye out for us as well. Years later, when I became a police reporter, many of those friendships remained, although the detectives never spoke much about the case. I knew, and they knew I knew.

One night Mother and I got home rather late from a movie and found that every light bulb in our yard and garage had been unscrewed. This gave us great concern and added intensely to our worry that I might be kidnapped. Mother was quite inexperienced with firearms, and unfortunately, discharged her automatic weapon into the cement-covered backyard and sounded forth a loud scream, which surely frightened all the neighbors.

Our closest neighbor, Mrs. Charles McAllister Wilcox, got her second-story window up in a hurry wanting to know what the trouble was.

The trouble in part was that Mother had the giggles at having a gun discharge so we were unable to give a satisfactory explanation to Mrs. Wilcox until the next day.

One would have thought things would have quieted down with time. Instead we continued getting kidnap threats. These threats were quite real. We received a number of letters over the course of several years. The FBI was notified in each case and they kept a close eye on all our correspondence, but Mother never revealed any of this to Grandfather. Since I was a child, it certainly was never a subject of news articles or big headlines, but everyone was most anxious to prevent such a thing from happening to me. All of our associates carried guns, and for a while, it seemed everyone around me carried a gun except me.

Grandfather made sure I had a toy shotgun. It did not stand up too well to my heavy use and eventually fell into pieces making it totally unusable. I took this loss very seriously and sent Grandfather a letter asking for a replacement.

Stephen L. R. McNichols, who later became both an FBI agent and Colorado governor, was our chauffeur. He also commanded a naval vessel in the Mediterranean during World War II. At one point during the war, General George Patton was on his ship and demanded to be put ashore at Tunisia. McNichols had to stand up to Patton and refuse his demand because there were German submarines in the area making it too dangerous to conduct a landing expedition.

Even going to school became a well-choreographed process due to these threats. I attended Dora Moore Elementary School in Denver the year of 1934-1935 where Jesse Hamilton was the principal and Veronica Speaker, whom I dearly loved, was the school secretary.

In the morning I was driven to school by the chauffeur. After school, the plan was for me to go to Veronica Speaker's office and wait for her to finish her work. She then brought me home in her Model A, which was a thrill. I sure thought it was a swell car and took great pleasure in riding in it.

Mother always drove Packard cars purchased from Mountain Motors in Denver. George Minor was the manager, and I delighted in the stories he told. The one about bulletproofing a car for Al Capone was my favorite. All the glass windows were multi-paned to make them bulletproof. Some of the windows were adapted to raise a couple of extra inches revealing a hole just the right size for a machine gun muzzle, and the back window could drop down entirely. The whole car was armor plated, and it had a police band scanner and a siren.

Ironically Grandfather never learned to drive a car, although in later years he did own a Pierce Arrow and a Packard. My grandmother was always the driver of her electric car, which she had a habit of getting stranded in because the battery would run low. Many a time she had to get help pushing the car back uphill from downtown Denver to their house on Gilpin Street.

Once when she was driving to the Denver Post to attend a post-election function on Champa Street, she hit a couple of pedestrians who had been celebrating their candidate's winning campaign. Their inebriated condition didn't lend itself to being taken too seriously by the hospital staff, but they did recover and didn't appear too worse for wear.

As a small boy, I rode in the back seat of Mother's car as she and Aunt Bertha drove over bricks and other portions of a home in North Denver that had been demolished by dynamite. The destruction of the house

Pauline Lehman in her electric car in Denver's City Park.

appeared to be the handiwork of the Mafia. Those were wild times as the Great Depression was nearing its end. Al Capone was thought to be behind much of the destruction and violence, which was how he had maintained his power and control over most of the bootlegging operations throughout the country since 1928. Although Prohibition was waning, by 1933 drinkers preferred untaxed, bootlegged liquor because it was cheaper and easier to buy.

After Mother's marriage to Henry J. Lucke, she and I moved to New York City where his law practice was located. I was enrolled at St. Bernard School for Boys in the fall of 1932 for my first year of primary school. However, by the following fall, Mother was in the process of getting a divorce, and we were back in Denver where I began attending Graland Country Day School. There I met one of my closest school chums, David Downs. He was the son of one of the partners of Gano-Downs, a high-end men's clothing store in downtown Denver. Dave has remained a great friend to this day.

Our favorite childhood occupation was playing with my toy soldiers all over the house on Pennsylvania Street, but our favorite battlefield was the living room carpet. David's mother died when he was quite young and while this was certainly a big disruption in his young life, it didn't affect our friendship. Throughout our youth, no matter what school we were attending, Dave and I would get together at each other's homes where we always found some kind of mischief or adventure to occupy us.

On one occasion, I led the way to where I knew Mother kept her gun. Dave was in great awe and quite concerned that I might accidentally pull the trigger. I was deeply impressed with this prized possession and quite proud to display it. I suppose Dave's anxiety was somewhat contagious because I remember carefully and quickly replacing it.

Dave married Vickie Miller, a classmate of mine from Dora Moore Elementary School. We have remained lifelong friends and still get together for lunch or dinner several times a year.

With my friends since childhood, Vickie and David Downs, in Denver for lunch in 2014.

Chapter Six

EVERGREEN

EACH SPRING GRANDFATHER, MOTHER, AUNT BERTHA, AND I loaded the car for the drive from Denver to Evergreen, where we spent the summers, not returning until the fall. This was a trip to another land and I delighted in it.

We would begin with a 50-pound ice block strapped to the front bumper bound for the icebox in the mountain house. Grandfather rode in the front seat with the goldfish bowl between his feet. Duggan rode in the back seat, washing Mike's face repeatedly for him all the way up the canyon.

Mother's hobby and career in the late 1920s was developing her real estate in Evergreen. This produced a series of six homes—our summer home along with five rental cabins—on six-and-one-half acres on Evergreen Hill.

One of our family friends was Alf M. Landon, the former governor of Kansas and the 1936 Republican nominee for president of the United States. He enjoyed staying in the mountains and always rented one of Mother's cabins to escape the summer heat of Kansas.

We had a lovely view across a large meadow that soon became Evergreen Lake when a dam was built to contain the waters flowing down from Upper Bear Creek.

Our home was surrounded by a rock wall with a wooden frame fence attached on top. The fence had to be painted frequently, and I usually got the job. The property was mostly lawn and dandelions, and if I wasn't careful, I would be assigned the job of mowing too. I often changed my nap locations so I couldn't be found. With distractions, such as the bands playing tunes like "Maria Alana" at establishments across the lake, it was a wonder I ever got that lawn cut.

At the Evergreen summerhouse in 1927 with my carpenter's tool kit—a favorite gift from my mother.

"Little Lehman" as my family called me, with my grandfather and my beloved Aunt Bertha, always in an apron.

With Grandfather in front of the fountain at Mother's home in Evergreen. Behind us lies the meadow with Upper Bear Creek flowing through it. A dam was built in 1928 to help control flooding from spring runoff of the winter snowmelt.

Grandfather, Mother, and me having a picnic on the banks of Bear Creek in Bear Creek Canyon.

Evergreen Hill with view of our summer home and the five guest cabins reflected in Evergreen Lake.

Newly-built Evergreen Dam on Bear Creek as it flowed through the mountain hamlet of Evergreen.

Mother's summer home on Evergreen Hill.

Me, age six or seven, taking time out from the job of painting the fence.

Years later as a reporter for the *Rocky Mountain News,* I reported on plans for a lavish lodge and restaurant with several dwelling units to be located atop Evergreen Hill, overlooking the lake and town. Although the land was acquired and architectural drawings rendered, the venture never got any further.

One of our neighbors by the name of Stransky had a few cattle that loved our green lawn. Aunt Bertha would get out in the yard and flap her apron at them, but Duggan was the real star. He loved to demonstrate his herding talents whenever the cows strayed onto our property.

There was a cesspool on the property with a wooden roof. Once we found one of the Stransky cows bawling loudly after it had wandered onto the roof causing it to cave in. This created quite a commotion in the neighborhood as help was rounded up to get the cow safely removed.

After several seasons, Mother hired a couple to live in the guesthouse over the garage. The lady was our housekeeper and her husband was a very good craftsman and kept everything in top notch repair. I especially liked him because he relieved me of my lawn mowing and painting duties.

During these summers spent in Evergreen, I became friends with a group of boys close to my age, and we had some great times together. Herman Olde owned the Texaco station and his son had a convertible, which he and I would take out and try to roll as we drove over the mountain roads. We were never successful at this endeavor, but we had great fun trying.

Don Brubenzer and Eddy Ott were two other cohorts. Attired in plaid shirts and corduroy trousers, sometimes denim overhauls, the three of us would take small treks up Upper Bear Creek Canyon to Troutdale or Mt. Evans Ranch.

One summer Mother was happily exercising her independence by relighting a butane-fired stove located in the basement. When it blew up, she was severely burned on her legs and arms. Since we didn't have a wheelchair, I pulled her around in a rocking chair during her recovery. I was also assigned responsibilities of chief cook, which resulted in a steady diet of hotdogs. The doctor came every day to remove Mother's bandages and replace them with fresh ones. Although I'm sure Mother's recovery was quite painful, the remarkable thing was she made it back to good health with not one scar.

When I finally got a day off, I went to Denver with Frank Castille, a local Evergreen realtor who was very good-natured. He owned the

Me with boyhood pals in Evergreen.

Fireside Café where I washed dishes during my junior high years and he drove me home when I was done. He later lost his life in a flood in Bear Creek Canyon.

This break from caring for Mother afforded me the opportunity to stock up on hamburgers and lemon meringue pie from the Rocky Built Café in Denver, but I paid a heavy price by getting the hives. Returning to Evergreen in bad shape, moaning and groaning from the terrible itching and completely unable to sleep, I received no consolation or sympathy from Mother.

Another time Mother was atop a horse in the middle of the road by our house. Her horse put his head down to the ground and she toppled over, face first onto the gravel. She was able to make it to the house and the doctor came and removed the gravel pieces bit by bit from her face. Once again, she had a remarkable recovery with no scarring.

On one memorable return trip to Denver in a downpour, Mother had trouble keeping the car on the road due to the bright lights of oncoming cars. She pulled off to the side of the road to avoid hitting them, but when she tried to pull back onto the road she went into a skid—with all the car's occupants, which included Mother, Grandfather, Mike, Duggan and me—going down into the ravine, just northwest of Morrison.

Once we got our bearings, the decision was made for me to go back up the hillside and flag down some help. As I stood to the side of the road, I attracted the attention of the night marshal in his Model A and soon we had a lot of help.

I got to use the siren the rest of the way down the canyon, which thrilled me, but Mike complained all the way. Whoever brought him back to the house in Denver put him downstairs, where he continued to complain.

I was checked for injuries at Denver General Hospital while the others went to Colorado General Hospital. Everyone checked out fairly well, but Grandfather was left with an arm injury causing severe arthritis that continually bothered him, all the way up to his death. Somehow the front seat was wedged perpendicular. How they got him out of the car and then up the side of the mountain to the road, I don't know.

The next day was the Bear Creek flood of 1933, which flooded Cherry Creek where the sunken gardens at the Denver Country Club sank even further.

EDWARD LEHMAN

1925 ~ 2018

Matthew 5:15-16 King James Version (KJV)

Neither do men light a candle, and put it under a bushel, but on a candlestick; and it giveth light unto all that are in the house.

Let your light so shine before men, that they may see your good works, and glorify your Father which is in heaven.

ROTARY MOTO
Service above Self

To build a better world, start in your own community.

In Loving Memory of

EDWARD LEHMAN

BORN
September 10, 1925
Denver, CO

PASSED AWAY
November 10, 2018
Longmont, CO

MEMORIAL SERVICE
Friday   November 16, 2018   11:00 AM
St. Stephen's Episcopal Church

OFFICIANT
Reverend Dana Solomon

SCRIPTURE READERS
Dean Lehman
Suzanne Barrett
Don Wood

SPEAKERS
Diane Stow
Dr. Al Carr
John Vahlenkamp

MUSIC
"Going Home"
"O' Loving God"
"The Lord's Prayer"
"O' God Our Help in Ages Past" ~ Congregational
"God Bless America" ~ Congregational
Robert Hjelmstad ~ Accompanist
Stephanie Kelly ~ Vocalist

Please join the family for a reception and brunch in Boone Hall immediately following the service for Ed.

God Bless America

God bless America, land that I love
Stand beside her and guide her
Through the night with the light from above
From the mountains to the prairies
To the oceans white with foam
God bless America, my home sweet home
God bless America, land that I love
Stand beside her and guide her
Through the night with the light from above
From the mountains to the prairies
To the oceans white with foam
God bless America, my home sweet home
From the mountains to the prairies
To the oceans white with foam
God bless America, my home sweet home
God bless America, my home sweet home

Please stand and join us in song honoring
Edward Lehman as the family exits the sanctuary

Chapter Seven

CUBA

IN 1933 GRANDFATHER, MOTHER AND I TRAVELED TO MIAMI, and then on to Havana, through the Panama Canal for the return trip. While this was a much-needed vacation for Mother and Grandfather, I suspected it was done to ensure my safety by getting me out of the country, if only for a short time.

Mother often discussed safety precautions with me so I was aware of these threats. Being a child I naturally was frightened by some of this activity—such as the safety precautions in getting to and from school; bedtime household security checks; and never being alone or unsupervised when outdoors—so I took all security procedures seriously. There also were times when they contained an element of great adventure and excitement, which has been my lifelong admiration and fascination with police and firemen. They kept a watchful eye out for me and I never will forget that.

We traveled by ship on the *President Harrison* and had adventures and experiences along the way. This was during the period when Fulgencio Batista was attempting to gain control of the government, so our visit to Cuba was somewhat strained. There was considerable turmoil as the government appeared to be in total chaos. We had two police officers protecting us and keeping us out of trouble by day, but the real excitement came when it was time to leave. We had to take a small boat to the *President Harrison* because the ship's captain refused to venture into the harbor to pick up passengers. Much later during World War II, the Japanese commandeered the *President Harrison*. It was converted into a Japanese troop ship but didn't fair too well and was eventually sunk by the United States.

At the age of eight, I easily made friends with the sailors and crew. This afforded me the advantage to go anywhere on board that I desired—

Prior to setting sail for Cuba in 1933, Mother and I had our picture taken. It was used as our passport identification.

from the radio room to the bridge and other areas not normally accessible to the traveling public.

We sailed through the Culebra Cut, formerly called the Gaillard Cut, an artificial valley that cut through the Continental Divide of Panama. As we passed through, the captain and crew on the bridge turned the controls over to me. They all seemed to think this was very funny for a young boy to be at the helm of this mighty ship. I must say the ship responded quite well to all my commands. What a grand time I had.

One deeply sad note for me was the death of Aunt Bertha from pneumonia at the age of 71 during that following winter. She had taken wonderful care of me, and we shared many adventures. I remember walks with her through our Denver neighborhood when I was very small. She always stopped to let me climb up and sit atop the cement lions guarding Molly Brown's home, one of my favorite things to do on our walks together.

With Aunt Bertha gone, Mother took me with her and Grandfather on one particular vacation to Miami. During this trip she enrolled me in the Riverside School for Boys for a couple of months. While she and Grandfather vacationed, she became acquainted with several real estate

During the late fall in 1933, I was hospitalized with pneumonia. I received many letters from my schoolmates, David Downs among them, wishing me a speedy recovery and hoping I didn't miss Santa.

men who were determined to get her to buy some property, specifically an island that had been owned by Al Capone. When that didn't bear any fruit, they attempted to sell her Al Capone's 1928 Cadillac. We never saw Mr. Capone because by this time he had been in prison for several years for tax evasion with most of his assets seized. We came to believe these real estate men were likely agents of Mr. Capone, trying to dispose of his remaining property. Fortunately Mother did not buy the island or the car, and we returned to Denver safely.

> Dec. Twenty-fourth
> Thirty-three
>
> Dear little Lehman,—
> Santa is very sorry you must spend Christmas in the hospital. As you had asked for a work-table and a switch and Track for your electric train

In fact, I received a letter from Santa.

San Francisco was another of Grandfather's favorite vacation spots. In 1935 while vacationing there, he became ill with pneumonia, so Mother and I traveled to California to be with him. We lived in various hotels, and I was enrolled at Damon School for Boys. My favorite part of each day was going to and from school by cable car while Mother took care of Grandfather.

We all managed to return to Denver, but a short time later at the age of 78, Grandfather succumbed to the pneumonia without any knowledge of the kidnap threats against me. It was just as well as he would have been terribly troubled by it all.

> and a few other things
> Santa had them de-
> livered to 920 Penn.
> and you will find them
> when you can go home
> Santa knows you
> are a very brave boy
> and he knows you
> will be much better
> in a day or two!
> Cant write any
> more for Time is short.
> Merry Xmas,
> Santa.

I began the 1936 fall school year at St. John's Lutheran School, but soon was transferred back to my old alma mater, Dora Moore, and remained there through 1938. I loved school there. My good school buddies and I addressed each other by our last names, such as Kirchoff (Francis), Marr (Art), Cornforth (Gene), and I was Lehman. I still have many notes my school chums sent me when I was sick.

Chapter Eight

MILITARY SCHOOL

I ATTENDED MOREY JUNIOR HIGH MY FIRST YEAR but the remainder of junior high was spent at Colorado Military School, located on Columbine Street, near Denver University. I was in the cavalry unit and we rode daily on an old dirt road that was a part of the Fairmount Cemetery, long before the mausoleum was developed.

We were directed by a group of retired cavalry officers who were fearless for us. The horse assigned to me was named Burt. I had to keep him reasonably presentable and we got along fairly well. However, a fellow cadet, who was somewhat overweight, did not have the same relationship with his mount. To even things up one day when he was in the process of mounting, his horse bit him right on the fanny. As he got off holding his aching rear, he delivered a punch to his horse's jaw, which resulted in demerits for striking his horse.

Later, in a practice cavalry charge, Garrett Van Holt led the assault superbly, until he fell off his horse. A cadet following close behind came along and his horse stepped right on Garrett's leg, fracturing it in several places. He was taken away by ambulance. Eventually when he returned on crutches, he was assigned a different horse.

High school began at Denver's East High, but at this stage of my life, I yearned for more freedom and independence and was quite eager to remove myself from my mother's ever watchful eyes. Latin and advanced math and the challenges that came with them provided the perfect excuse for making the transfer to St. John's Military School (SJMS) in Salina, Kansas. The experiences I had during the years I spent at St. John's are some of my fondest memories. Traveling between Salina and Denver by

I graduated from St. John's Military School in the class of 1943.

train during summers, holidays, and mid-term breaks cemented my lifelong love for train travel.

A mock battle staged between the Fort Riley Motorized Infantry and St. John's Cadets took place in the spring of 1943 in Salina. The town's citizenry soon became aware of what was going on and turned out to observe the ensuing battle. It got off to an amazing start when we loaded some of our blank shells and shot Fort Riley's lead gunner in the face. He was bleeding profusely and had to get off their motorized gun. He became one of the first true casualties of the battle. We also had a number of small sandbag traps in odd places and smoke bombs.

Much to the Fort Riley infantry's surprise, they discovered we had let the air out of the tires on some of their vehicles, which contributed in stopping their forward momentum completely. The battle began to develop into fights in the old main barracks that included water with fire hoses. The Fort Riley infantry also did not hesitate to shove the furniture around. They were quite surprised when the SJMS cadets were equally, if not more, eager to shove the furniture right back. Of course, the public was unaware of this behind-the-scenes battle.

A few years after I graduated from St. John's Military School this grand old building, which was the main headquarters, was destroyed by fire.

We turned a number of non-combatants into casualties. Many of them had quite a long wait to be picked up and taken for first aid because we needed every able bodied person we could muster to win the battle.

My role as a platoon sergeant kept me busy directing fortification of buildings and areas under our control. It was a continuous mobile battle everywhere once we got going. Referees from the Fort Riley Infantry declared the SJMS cadets the winners because of our ingenuity in fighting off the infantry.

During my senior year I was quartermaster in charge of lots of old World War 1 uniforms. In fact, without too much trouble we all could have looked like Army cadets. I was also on the fencing team where we were limited to competition at the college level. We never lost a match.

The best job I had was being a platoon sergeant. I had a ranking officer named Connie Eastman, who later became a Lieutenant Colonel in World War II. He was a big guy and always in some kind of hot water with the superintendent of administration at St. John's, but I thoroughly enjoyed him.

At about age 16 I got a summer job as a paperboy for the *Denver Post*, further reinforcing my early symptoms of "printer's ink in the veins." What I remember most was meeting the milkman. People would move out on him and he wouldn't get paid and I wouldn't get paid, so we got to know each other pretty well. It was just a great experience. I met a lot of people who were really very, very nice and some who were very, very ornery, and they had terrible memories. They couldn't remember to pay you, even though you made five and six efforts at collecting. That was before they moved out in the middle of the night, but I would be glad for this experience later in life.

In January of my last semester at St. John's, at Mother's insistence, I traveled to Braden's West Point Prep School in Cornwall-on-Hudson, New York, to bone up on English and math. At the time I didn't think much of this phase in my schooling, but after returning to Salina, I successfully graduated from St. John's, making the journey to New York worth the time and effort.

Over the years, I have attended several of St. John's Military School commencement ceremonies. I was invited to speak at one of them where my statement to the graduating corps was, "Guiding and living your life is no spectator sport. Set your goals and determine to make good things happen. Only you can do it, and SJMS gives you a wonderful start."

Me in 1946 while attending DU and working for the Rocky Mountain News.

Chapter Nine

DU AND THE ROCKY MOUNTAIN NEWS YEARS

THE SUMMER AFTER GRADUATION, once again at Mother's urging, I spent my spare moments on a project of special interest to her. When Grandfather owned his jewelry store in Denver, he had ordered service jewelry during World War I. These were quite popular with soldiers' families, but when the war ended abruptly, he was left with a sizeable inventory that was no longer marketable.

I wasn't particularly interested in this project, but I was obedient to Mother and went to work setting up my vice and removing the precious gems from the settings. I worked on and off on this project most of the summer until it was completed. The new owners of the jewelry store were quite surprised to receive these gems and Mother was thrilled to have this bit of unfinished business from the sale of the jewelry store completed.

With my popularity with Mother at an all-time high, I headed off to Denver University, where I attended through 1947, receiving a B.A. in political science. When I first began my studies, I used to catch the #8 trolley from near my home on Pennsylvania Street to the university campus. This trolley soon had the nickname "Tramway Tech" because it dropped off passengers, many of whom were students at DU, at the old sports stadium.

A great old institution called the Stadium Inn became a meeting center where students could drink beer and smoke pipes as they waited for the trolley. Those were some grand times, and many wonderful friendships were forged.

While attending DU, I moonlighted as a police reporter for the *Rocky Mountain News*. I got the job because a friend of mine, Art Holch—whose father, Art Holch Sr., was a DU faculty member—did not want to contin-

In the newsroom of the Rocky Mountain News *where I worked from 1945 to 1947. (Rocky Mountain News Photo)*

ue his position as police reporter with the daily assortment of rough experiences that were part of the job. And, it was endless. I was always grateful to Art for vacating this position that others sought to fill. I relished my work at the *Rocky Mountain News* all through my college years. Studying journalism in college never occurred to me. I was working forty hours a week at it. It just seemed to me that I was getting my education in the college of actual practice.

In those days the newspaper industry's philosophy was learning by doing. They trained their own people and did a darn good job. A rookie started with "rewrite jobs" involving massaging stories into publishable form from copy phoned in by reporters. It was tough training from tough-minded people.

Journalism degrees were a rare commodity among working journalists when editor and publisher Jack Foster hired me in 1945. My first editor, Bob Chase, was married to Mary Coyle Chase, also a veteran Denver newspaper professional. Mary Coyle Chase wrote *Harvey*, a popular comedy about an imaginary rabbit that opened on Broadway in 1944. Later adapted for film in 1950, it starred James Stewart and Josephine Hull. A 1970 Broadway revival production of the play starred James Stewart and Helen Hayes.

I sometimes had to call Bob at home on Saturdays because he and Mary usually didn't come into the newsroom until quite a bit later in the afternoon. I've often wondered how many times I must have interrupted the writing of *Harvey*.

I had responsibility for reporting on what was termed the "federal run," which consisted of the U.S. Post Office under the supervision of James O. Stevic; the Pure Food and Drug Administration (PFDA), whose chief investigator was J. L. White; the Alcohol and Tax Unit (ATU); the U.S. Marshall's Office; and the federal court, which involved presentation of narcotics cases and other illicit crimes. I made daily visits to each of these agencies to gather updated information on developing news stories and pick up leads on any new investigations.

When the FBI was a relatively new organization, any local contact with news outlets had to be approved by FBI Director J. Edgar Hoover. R. D. Brown headed up the Colorado FBI during this period and was held in high regard by all law enforcement agencies, both local and national. I had gotten to know him quite well as a child, which afforded me unusual access and contacts within the FBI. The contacts were very helpful when Brown was later supplanted by a new agent in charge, R. P. Kramer.

The Elitch Gardens fire of 1944. (Rocky Mountain News Photo)

Chapter Ten

FIRES AND GAMBLING

MY MANY ADVENTURES AS A REPORTER made for some unforgettable days and nights. They also kept Mother entertained. She always made sure to sit up and welcome me when I got home because she did not want to miss any of the juicy details of the breaking stories of the day.

I loved newspaper reporting. I found it very interesting and found that being a longtime native gave me a certain advantage. I knew many of the people who were on their way up. Take Jim Childers who was chief detective and later chief of police. I remembered him from when he directed traffic at 16th and Broadway. Working on papers in Denver, I had a certain advantage having been a part of three generations in Denver. I knew where the stories were and often what the stories *behind* the stories were.

Gosh! Denver was an exciting town. There were many, many stories. Later I had an arrangement where I would be notified on multiple alarm fires. One year I think I got twelve multiple alarm fire calls. Folks from the paper would come to DU and get me when there was a fire. One of my great interests has always been firefighting. I spent a lot of time with firemen. I just enjoyed them and appreciated what they did. I was interested in their equipment and everything about their work.

During the time when I was a fire and police reporter, I covered several four-alarm fires with the Denver Fire Department. Four were especially memorable. They were the Elitch Gardens Old Mill fire, the Denver Dry Goods warehouse fire, the Park Lane Hotel fire, and a huge fire that covered many acres at Fort Carson near Colorado Springs.

One Sunday afternoon in mid-July 1944 as three boatloads of people were going through the dark and winding tunnel of the Old Mill building at the Elitch Gardens, a flash fire broke out. The rapid buildup of smoke caused two soldiers, their wives, and two attendants to die of suffocation. Within a very short time, the flames moved to the exterior of the building, engulfing the front portico.

Mr. Gurtler, manager of Elitch Gardens, thought the Old Mill was one of the safest attractions at the park. Although the cause was never officially declared, the source was thought to have been in the electrical wiring.

Another fire in downtown Denver at the Denver Dry Goods warehouse quickly became a three-alarm fire. *Rocky Mountain News* photographer Harry M. Rhoads and I hurried up to the top of the Daniels & Fisher Tower to get a better view. This became our lookout for future downtown fires as it gave us the highest vantage point in downtown Denver at that time.

Rescue operations underway at the 1944 Elitch Gardens fire.
(Rocky Mountain News Photo)

Chief John F. Healy of the Denver Fire Department arrived after the third alarm to lend a hand. Finding quite a number of firefighters overcome by smoke, he first ordered a pole from one of the fire trucks taken around to the back of the building and used as a ramrod to open up the double doors to let the smoke escape from the warehouse. He then sent his driver to *Bijou's*, a downtown Denver bar just across the street from the Brown Palace Hotel, for some bourbon for the firefighters. This seemed to help the situation considerably.

Another fire that stands out vividly in my memory was due substantially more to a hair-raising journey on the ladder than the fire itself. Rhoads and I brought up the rear behind Chief Healy, who in his late sixties or early seventies, led us up a tremendous ladder attached to the hook and ladder truck. I figured if the Chief could do it, so could I as we began the ascent. Completely occupied with carrying Harry's bag of cameras and photo gear, I did not fully appreciate the situation I was getting into. Once Harry had gotten the shots he wanted, and it was time for the return trip, the full realization of how high we actually were hit me full force.

As it turned out, going down the ladder was the most terrifying part of the experience. I didn't dare look down or I would have been frozen to the spot. Quite honestly, I have very little recollection of how I got back down that ladder. I do remember the return trip took at least two or three times longer than going up. I never climbed another ladder like it again, but I have never forgotten that brief "bird's eye" view.

The fire at the Park Lane Hotel, located on South Marion Street, was considered rather spectacular at the time. About all I remember of it was my attempt to talk a woman out of dropping her radio to the ground from several floors up. However, I was unsuccessful and when the radio hit the ground it broke into bits and pieces, just as I had told her it would.

A much larger fire took place at Camp Carson on what is now the Fort Carson army base just south of Colorado Springs. The fire covered a large number of acres due to extremely high winds, which led to the destruction of some of the barracks before the firemen were able to get it under control. When we arrived to cover the story, firefighting efforts were well under way, but the firemen were having quite a hard time fighting it.

On the world scene, President Franklin Roosevelt had just been elected to his fourth term. One of his first meetings was with British Prime Minister Winston Churchill and Soviet Premier Joseph Stalin in Yalta to

I covered everything from automobile accidents to fires and shootings for the Rocky Mountain News. *Here I interviewed witnesses to a traffic accident involving a school bus in May 1947. (Rocky Mountain News Photo)*

map out post-war Europe. Within a couple of months, Roosevelt would be dead, but the war was not completely over yet. Fighting would continue in the Pacific, finally ending by mid-summer when Japan surrendered after atomic bombs were dropped on Hiroshima and Nagasaki. Fighting continued in China, Burma, and India until the late fall of 1945.

Closer to home, during the spring and summer of 1946, I wrote several articles dealing with gambling in and around the Denver area. There had been a bold holdup in early March by thirteen armed robbers at the swank Wolhurst Saddle Club, located in rural Douglas County. The robbery netted more than $20,000 in money and jewels taken from the customers. There was an establishment loss as well, which was thought to be exceedingly heavy, but more importantly, the robbery exposed the whole gambling operation.

Although the gaming equipment was seized and the operation shut down, the operators of Wolhurst, O. E. (Smiling Charlie) Stephens and Eddie Jordan, his nephew and partner, appeared to have left the state with warrants for their arrest still in the hands of Douglas County Sheriff H. R. (Bob) Campbell. The gaming equipment could not be destroyed because it had to be held as evidence in the event these two ever came to trial.

Interestingly, during the grand jury inquiry into the Wolhurst holdup, it came out that Stephens was actually living near Louisville and making frequent trips into Denver for pre-arranged meetings with the more than thirty patron-victims for the purpose of covering the losses claimed in the robbery. Amazingly, these losses were meticulously detailed by Eddie Jordan just minutes after the robbers had left the scene of the holdup. One claim of diamond-studded jewelry valued at a fantastically high figure reportedly was still in the negotiating stage.

Continued sightings of Stephens were reported in such disparate locations as Phoenix, Arizona, and Hot Springs, Arkansas. Other information indicated he was headquartering in Omaha, Nebraska, where he was known to have some of his prize racehorses stabled. It was thought the likely enticement keeping Stephens close to Colorado was his string of valuable thoroughbred horses, which were still kept at the Wolhurst club for the use of its members. Many of these horses had won top honors in the National Western Stock Show.

Another thought-provoking aspect to this case was the surreptitious behavior of the patrons who had been robbed. None of them were ever identified. To a person they all covered their heads upon entering or leaving meeting destinations. The paper would get license numbers but often the patrons had used borrowed vehicles. We simply lacked the sophistication in probing public records and in every case were unsuccessful in tracking down their true identities.

Colorado Springs District Attorney Irl Foard appointed a former Denver police sergeant, Lawrence F. Stone, as special investigator, but to my knowledge, the case never came to trial.

Meanwhile, by mid-August a new rendezvous on one of the main streets in Idaho Springs was being established for the benefit of some members of the Wolhurst Saddle Club. One warm evening a number of cars bearing Denver licenses were seen parked on the streets outside a particular establishment and the affable and opulent "Squire of Wolhurst," O. E. Stephens, was seen walking on the street close by.

This brought a Clear Creek County official to town to investigate. When he attempted to enter the gambling establishment, he was turned away by a well-known Denver lawyer who demanded that he show a search warrant. Judging from the voices coming from inside, a game of chance was in full sway. The next day, however, only a plush carpet and a Denver man with a bland expression greeted a Rocky Mountain News reporter when he entered the place.

The Sheriff of Clear Creek County at the time, Harold N. Brumbaugh, reported he thoroughly investigated the district after reading the exposé in the *Rocky Mountain News*. He and his chief deputy, Charles Hull, had also investigated reports of a fairly large "mystery club" operating in nearby Soda Creek or Chicago Creek Canyon. After spending several nights planted in these areas and finding no traces of the reported activity, they concluded there was no longer any gambling taking place in Idaho Springs.

Also as a result of the *Rocky Mountain News* article, Brumbaugh and Hull conferred behind closed doors with Erl H. Ellis, deputy district attorney, and upon adjournment, they announced that slot machines were being banned thenceforth in Idaho Springs. Brumbaugh and Hull were assigned to visit every establishment where slots had been in operation, estimated to be around 150 scattered throughout the town. The machines were owned by the operators of the establishments and the "take" had been divided with half going to veterans' organizations and the other half used for various civic enterprises.

Many of the townsfolk felt the articles in the paper had scared off any outside big-time gambling planning to come into Idaho Springs, and they were relieved. However, they were disappointed in seeing the slot machines vanish because these had been used to collect funds for worthy community projects and under the control of the town. Not surprisingly, this was not the end of gambling. It would be revisited in the future. Although some of the faces and names would change, many of the locations would be the same.

Chapter Eleven

RAILROADED AT UNION STATION

THE SUMMER AND FALL OF 1946 turned out to be quite a "hot time in the old town" of Denver. On the morning of June 20, at 6:30, a shooting took place at the portals of Denver's Union Railroad Station, leaving a 35-year-old Kearney, Nebraska, Army Air Force veteran, William L. Cross, dead by the hand of a well-regarded, eight-year veteran of the Denver Police Department, Frank D. Cowgill.

The day of the killing District Attorney James T. Burke broke precedent and entered personally into the investigation of the slaying. Burke appeared at police headquarters at 5:00 p.m. while police and Deputy District Attorney Joseph A. Myers were questioning Patrolman Cowgill.

Burke pointed out on his arrival he was appearing at the inquiry "only to get a first-hand picture of this situation. The fact that a fully-armed patrolman, apparently drunk and in full uniform, is involved in a cold-blooded killing necessitates my personal attention."

Police investigators, under the direction of Detective Captain James E. Childers, determined Cross's death climaxed an all-night drinking spree precipitated by the Louis-Conn boxing match.

At the age of twenty-one, I found myself covering what would become a significant murder trial. It began October 19 at West Side Court in an atmosphere of bathos. During the selection process, the jury seemed more interested in the outcome of the final game of the World Series than in the fact that they might sit in judgment of Frank D. Cowgill, a 36-year-old Denver policeman, on trial for his life.

There was pathos, too. Cowgill, his eyes red-rimmed from emotion that frequently got the best of him, sat at the defense table. His eyes were downcast to the floor in front of him. He wrung his hands again and again. Behind him, in the front row of spectator seats, sat his wife, Marguerite Cowgill, 33, her tear-swollen eyes often hidden behind a pair of sunglasses. Choked sobs occasionally broke from the lips of the couple's two oldest children Margie Cowgill, 14, and Frank Cowgill Jr., 10, who sat beside their mother. Judith Cowgill, five, sat on her mother's lap apparently oblivious of the tense drama that began to unfold in the courtroom. Occasionally she pointed a chubby finger toward her father, who kept his eyes away from the grief-stricken family. Also in attendance were Cowgill's parents, Ralph and Sara Cowgill, who came to Denver from Los Angeles to be with their son.

The trial got under way in earnest after District Judge Robert W. Steele called a recess at 3:00 p.m. and announced the final score of the World Series game to the packed courtroom.

The hearing for the murder charge also touched off a month-long grand jury examination of alleged police irregularities called at the request of District Attorney Burke.

Deputy District Attorney Joseph A. Myers and his assistant, Charles E. Grover, posed the usual grim questions of a murder trial to the prospective jurors. They repeatedly asked juror after juror if they objected to capital punishment.

With equal deliberation, defense attorneys Frederick E. Dickerson and Anthony F. Zarlengo, propounded questions concerning acts committed by insane persons and the feeling of prospective jurors toward pleas of insanity. "You realize," Dickerson asked one prospective juror, "that if you determine that a man was insane at the time he committed a crime, and sane now, that under Colorado law he must be confined in an institution?" The question brought vigorous protest from Myers, who asked for a hearing on the question in Judge Steele's chambers. The court overruled the protest and held with Dickerson.

During intermission, Cowgill conferred with his family and broke down in tears when his youngest daughter, Judith, asked him where he had been. Cowgill had been held in County Jail since the June 20 slaying.

Cowgill said he did not remember any of his actions for several hours preceding the shooting and pleaded not guilty by reason of insanity to the charges when arraigned in August. He was placed under observation for fifteen days at Colorado Psychopathic Hospital. Dr. Franklin G. Ebaugh, director of the hospital, and his associate, Dr. Stuart K. Bush, pronounced Cowgill sane "now and at the time of the shooting."

Childers testified Cowgill told him of getting into his car with Patrolmen William H. McNulty and Sam Tangye after duty on the night of June 19, and making the rounds of several North Denver taverns and drive-ins. They said Cowgill at first refused to join in the drinking but later helped consume several fifths of whisky. Childers told the court that Cowgill said the last event of the night he recalled was a visit to the 800 block of Santa Fe Drive and that he remembered nothing until he was arrested with a smoking revolver in his hand. A courtroom battle developed between opposing attorneys over two sets of photographs of Cowgill, one taken by police and the other by Harry M. Rhoads, *Rocky Mountain News* photographer. The police photos show Cowgill as neat and sober with his hair combed. Rhoads' news pictures, taken the afternoon of June 20, expose Cowgill as a gaunt, disheveled, and wild-eyed man with hair awry. Childers testified the police photos showed Cowgill as he appeared shortly after the shooting.

Earlier, Patrolman R. R. Richardson testified Cowgill was "out of this world" from drink when he overpowered and arrested him in the street in front of Union Station. "I believe this man was insane at the time of the shooting," Richardson told the court. He testified that in more than twenty years of service as a patrolman he had only once before seen the expression he saw on Cowgill's face when he disarmed and arrested him—that was when he arrested a West Denver man who had just killed his mother. That man was sent to the Colorado State Hospital, he testified.

Richardson displayed to the jury a scar on his right hand from a wound suffered as the hammer of Cowgill's revolver bit into his flesh as he disarmed him. He described Cowgill as vague, incoherent, and mumbling when arrested, and told the court, "He mumbled something about *'Did we get 'em?'* and tried to say something about a stickup."

Following Richardson's testimony, Chief Deputy District Attorney Joseph A. Myers sought to lay grounds for impeachment of the witness on grounds he had changed his statements made at earlier hearings into the killing. He claimed "surprise" testimony as a legal move in order to extend the scope of his cross-questioning of Richardson. Judge Robert W. Steele granted his motion.

Cowgill sat quietly throughout the testimony with his head dejectedly in his hands.

Frank D. Cowgill, during my jail interview with him August 22, 1946. (Rocky Mountain News Photo)

Throughout the testimony there were sharp exchanges between Myers and Defense Attorney Dickerson. At one point Dickerson accused Myers of "trying to put blood all over the place" in his questioning and statements.

The state rested its case after testimony from Detective Michael Rafrone, Police Identification Bureau expert, on Cowgill's sobriety and mental condition at the time the police photograph was made.

For the first time in the history of West Side Court, counsel for a defendant charged with murder rested their case abruptly without presenting a bit of evidence. This totally unexpected move came when Defense Attorneys Frederick Dickerson and Anthony Zarlengo announced the defense would rest. "Our defense already has been presented and proved by the state," Dickerson said in brief explanation. "Three of their [the prosecution's] witnesses testified that Cowgill was insane when he killed William Cross. That's been our contention all the time."

Dickerson and Zarlengo also said that a graphic story of Cowgill's condition had been told in the *Rocky Mountain News* photos, which had been presented as evidence by the state.

"It's plain to see from the pictures that the testimony of three state witnesses about Cowgill's sanity was correct," Dickerson added. "Patrolman R. R. Richardson told how Cowgill was 'crazy' when he disarmed him. Officer Philip Gartland described Cowgill as a 'walking ghost' from liquor only 30 minutes before the shooting. And Cowgill's partner, Patrolman William McNulty, said he was 'totally nuts.' That's good enough for us. It presents our case."

"Our main witness would have been Cowgill and he was in no shape to testify," Zarlengo added. "Earlier ... when Patrolman Fred Broderius took the stand and testified with tears in his eyes how he had been called to the murder scene and arrested Cowgill, his lifelong friend, Cowgill couldn't even remember ever having known him."

The case went to the jury the next morning.

This was the first time in Denver jurisprudence that defense attorneys took such a chance with a murder case. It had been twenty-four years since that technique was used in a lesser case. It was in the same courtroom in 1922 during the famed trial of twenty-two defendants in the Lou Blonger "bunko ring" case that attorneys took a similar chance. However, in that case the defendants all were found guilty.

Joseph Myers immediately requested District Judge Robert W. Steele to permit the state to present testimony of psychiatrists, who had been held in reserve for rebuttal after the defense rested.

Judge Steele ruled the further evidence would not be permissible because no defense evidence had been presented to refute. Previously, some had predicted the trial would end in a "battle of psychiatrists" as to the sanity of Cowgill.

Mrs. Cross had come to Denver from Nebraska for the trial. She and her late husband had four children—ages three to sixteen. She said she "tried hard to think rationally" about how her husband was killed after being wounded twice by Cowgill in an unexplained shooting which climaxed a night-long drinking spree.

On October 26 Frank D. Cowgill was acquitted of the murder of William L. Cross by reason of insanity.

Many felt there had been a disgraceful miscarriage of justice, including the *Rocky Mountain News*. Lee Casey, news editor, wrote in the October 26 edition that blame for the acquittal should be placed directly at the door of District Attorney Burke, whom he thought should have tried Frank D. Cowgill personally.

Of equal importance in my mind—especially after interviewing Mr. Cowgill in August—was the complete lack of proof of insanity. There was no question that Mr. Cowgill was under the influence of alcohol and was not behaving in a responsible manner toward his colleagues as well as the victim, who was only a first-time acquaintance. But did his behavior in those early morning hours immediately preceding the shooting meet the requirements for insanity?

Joseph A. Myers, chief deputy district attorney, who handled the case in the absence of Mr. Burke, didn't offer any proof of Mr. Cowgill's sanity during the trial. Instead of calling experts to the stand, he kept back testimony of state psychiatrists to use in rebuttal. But the defense did not offer that line of evidence and so the state through its inexplicable lack of foresight never had a chance. Instead the citizens of Denver were left with the most perplexing phenomenon of a man being declared insane—or, rather, not guilty by reason of insanity—without any expert testimony being taken.

F. E. Dickerson and Anthony F. Zarlengo, two of the ablest defense and trial attorneys of the Denver bar, saw early on that the prosecution was presenting a marvelous defense for them. They simply took advantage of the gift.

In the end Frank D. Cowgill did spend time at the State Psychiatric Hospital in Pueblo. He and his family moved to Pueblo permanently where he died in his mid-70s in 1984.

Chapter Twelve

A SECRET SERVICE AGENT'S SERVICE TO COLORADO

ONE OF MY MORE UNUSUAL ASSIGNMENTS WAS COVERING the retirement of Rowland K. Goddard, who was closing out nearly a half century of crime fighting in Colorado—just one state in his jurisdiction of a vast area of the West that included Wyoming, Utah, and Idaho.

As he prepared to retire at age seventy after forty-six years with the service, he recalled details of two of his highest profile cases:

A "lucky hunch" and some fast work paid dividends when he solved a $65,000 theft hundreds of miles from the crime scene and before the loss was discovered.

During his decades as an agent, he learned that when the telephone rang while he was eating dinner it usually meant trouble. This certainly was the case on a winter night in 1918. The caller was an excited pawnbroker who stuttered something about a well-dressed drunken man wanting to buy an expensive diamond ring with a $1,000 bond.

Goddard said he went right down to the pawnbroker's establishment and got a description of the man and the name he gave in the transaction. Fortunately, the pawnbroker had an office boy follow the suspect to a downtown hotel where he learned his room number by watching the suspect call for his key.

Goddard went to the hotel where he quizzed the night clerk and learned the man was intoxicated. He hurried to the room and knocked. It was then Goddard played his lucky hunch as the handsome man, obviously under the effects of alcohol, slowly opened the door.

Goddard demanded, "I'm an officer, where's the stuff?"

Rowland K. Goddard, left, retiring supervising agent of the Secret Service in Denver and his successor, Russell (Buck) Daniel. (Rocky Mountain News)

"Right over there," the man answered, pointing to a hand-tooled leather valise in a corner.

Goddard opened the satchel and found a sheaf of $1,000 government bonds, two large diamond rings, and almost $1,500 in cash. There were sixty-two bonds, indicating some had been spent. Goddard wired the

Federal Reserve Bank at Dallas, where the bonds were issued, and requested a check be made to see if any bonds were missing. During questioning, the suspect told Goddard he was a collateral clerk at the bank and admitted absconding with the $65,000 to "go on a bender."

Less than two years later in another case Goddard recovered more than $80,000 taken by Orville Harrington, a Denver Mint employee, before officials ever missed it.

According to Goddard, "[I] got the tip from someone who became suspicious of Harrington and suggested I watch him. Those were the days when Denver's Mint handled almost two million dollars a year in its gold refinery. Harrington was one of 33 men who worked there. If he hadn't become greedy he could easily have taken $75,000 and probably never been caught."

Goddard continued: "Harrington had a wooden leg and walked with a decided limp. This permitted his clothes to sag on the left side without anyone becoming suspicious. In that sag, Harrington carried out almost $80,000 in pure gold.

"Harrington gradually 'sneaked' the gold anodes out of the mint for months and took them to his South Denver home where he bricked up $75,000 worth of the precious metal in his basement." "He told us later he planned to just sit tight until the following June when the refinery closed down for an annual audit. But he couldn't wait. That was his weakness."

Goddard blamed Harrington's greed for his downfall. A fellow worker saw him wrap a gold bar with a cloth and then act as if he were going to slip it into his clothes. He replaced it when he saw he was being watched. His co-worker reported the incident. Goddard personally took the case.

He stated, "It was one of the fastest breaking cases I ever worked on. A night later, while I was hidden in a vacant lot watching his house, I saw Harrington come out with a coal bucket and bury something heavy in the backyard. That was the 'tip-off.'"

The next night, Goddard stepped from the shadows of a store building at 15th and Court Place and arrested Harrington. Inside his specially designed vest was another gold bar.

"Please shoot me," Harrington begged Goddard.

A few hours later, Goddard and his agents returned Harrington to his home. By the light of the moon, they went to the backyard where they dug up the garden and uncovered a $3,800 bar of gleaming gold. Goddard and his men rolled up their sleeves and broke out the false brick wall to recover $75,000 in carefully stacked gold bricks.

Further investigation revealed Harrington had taken a lease on a mine tunnel and planned to open an assay office in Cripple Creek, thus giving him a legitimate outlet for the stolen gold.

"He got ten years imprisonment," Goddard added.

Soon after Harrington was paroled from prison he returned to Denver but vanished mysteriously a short time later, never to be heard from again.

Chapter Thirteen

SOUTHERN COLORADO BANK ROBBERIES

IN COVERING THE FEDERAL RUN I became interested in some of the stories behind the stories, so I wrote two feature articles about Colorado bank robberies between 1928 and 1938. These robberies stood out in southern Colorado history and in the history of the West.

The first was a spectacular bank robbery that took place on May 23, 1928, at the First National Bank of Lamar. When it was over, the bandits had escaped with $238,000, the bank president and his son were dead, and two of the tellers had been taken hostage. Within a few hours the townspeople formed a posse and National Guard airplanes equipped with machine guns were flown to the area from Denver. Law enforcement officials throughout a three-state area joined in the manhunt for the four unmasked bandits. The gang left a trail of death behind them in southern Colorado and western Kansas, but one fingerprint would be the downfall of the last member of the gang to be brought to justice.

The leader was Ralph Fleagle, who as a farm boy had idolized Jesse James, the notorious Midwest outlaw. After the robbery and murders, Fleagle, along with his brother Jake and their two partners in crime, drove a short distance out of Lamar and released one of the bank cashiers, E. A. Lundgren, due to crowded conditions in the car. Lundgren reported to officers he felt the bandits were local because one of them had made a remark about the bank president, "I'm glad we got that old _____. He trimmed me on a land deal."

The gang then drove to Trinidad where they attempted to get the drug store proprietor to accompany them to treat a wounded pal supposedly injured in an accident. When she refused to go along, they departed.

This confirmed the officers' suspicions that one of the bandits was wounded by a bullet fired by the bank president just before he was killed. Ironically, the gun the bank president used had been a gift from a friend who had gotten it from Jesse James.

By 10:30 the night of the robbery, after successfully eluding capture, the gang had crossed into Kansas and one of them telephoned the home of Dr. W. W. Wineinger of Dighton, requesting the doctor come to a nearby farm to treat a man seriously injured in a tractor accident. Dr. Wineinger drove his car to the appointed place. That was the last time he was seen alive.

The robbers' trail became cold. Residents of the Rocky Mountain area were terrorized and farmers in the Smoky Hill district of Kansas demanded armed protection.

With each passing day, fear was growing for the safety of Dr. Wineinger. Then a scout plane sighted his car about 2.5 miles south of Oakley, Kansas, where it apparently had been pushed from the road. A posse hurried to the scene only to find the body of the doctor near his car where he had been slain by a blast from a shotgun, most likely only a few hours before their arrival.

A lone fingerprint was discovered when investigators searched the car for clues. It was sent to the National Division of Identification of the federal government, later to be known as the FBI. All clerks at the National Division of Identification were instructed to be on the lookout for a fingerprint matching the peculiar markings of the smudgy print found on the side of Wineinger's car.

More than a year passed before the print was identified as that of Jake Fleagle. The same day the prints were identified, law enforcement arrested Jake Fleagle Sr., father of the notorious brothers, for questioning. When he was arrested at his swank "horseless horse farm" near Garden City, Kansas, he claimed he had no knowledge of his sons' activities and told officers of their whereabouts. Ralph Fleagle was arrested a week later in Kankakee, Illinois. Under questioning he confessed to the Lamar bank holdup and named his brother Jake, Howard L. Royston, and G. J. Abshier as his associates. He also gave details of numerous other robberies they had been involved in throughout the West.

In August, Abshier was arrested in Cañon City living literally in the shadows of the gallows where he would eventually meet his death. A day later Royston was arrested in San Andreas, California, and rushed back to Colorado where he confessed to the Lamar robbery.

Southern Colorado and Western Kansas residents were terrorized by the notorious Fleagle outlaw gang in the late 1920s. The gang left a trail of death behind them after their daring daylight hold-up of the First National Bank of Lamar. One fatal fingerprint brought the last of the gang to justice. (Rocky Mountain News Feature Article)

By October the three were facing their trials in the Prowers County Courthouse in Lamar. One by one, each was found guilty of murder and sentenced to death. They were moved to Cañon City and placed in the death cell. To the very end, they told reporters there was no ill will between them even though Ralph Fleagle had identified them, believing he would receive a lighter sentence in return.

One mystery that remained unsolved was the vast sums of money deposited in various Kansas banks by the Fleagles. Officials of the Internal Revenue Service unsuccessfully questioned Ralph Fleagle about this. It is believed the money was the plunder of a life of crime engaged in by the Fleagle brothers.

Warden Francis E. Warren reported Ralph Fleagle died calmly the night of July 10, 1930. Nine days later Abshier and Royston, who had been school chums in Richmond, California, went calmly to their deaths.

Shortly before his brother's execution, Jake Fleagle boldly wrote letters to state and government officials offering to turn himself in, in return for a reversal of Ralph Fleagle's death sentence. The letters went unanswered.

As law enforcement agencies massed their combined strengths to capture Jake Fleagle, who was now also suspected of a California mail train robbery, federal agents were brought into the case.

After careful analysis of Jake's letters, postal authorities were alerted to watch for mail bearing his handwriting. Meanwhile, police placed a series of carefully worded ads in the personal columns of Kansas newspapers, bluffing Fleagle into thinking he was corresponding with an old friend who was an ex-convict. The old friend actually was under arrest and being used as a decoy. His name was never revealed.

It was known that Fleagle made frequent trips to San Jose, California, where he hid out when he wasn't in the Ozark Mountains. Over time his communication with the decoy led to planning a bank robbery. Fleagle planned to meet his accomplice in Yellville, Arkansas, to rob a Marion County bank. Agents infiltrated the entire area and waited.

On October 14, 1930, Jake Fleagle was spotted on a station platform in Branson, Missouri. When he climbed aboard an eastbound train and took his seat in a passenger car, he realized he was surrounded. With a gun in each hand, he jumped to his feet but was shot in the stomach before he could fire a single bullet.

A day later, Fleagle died in a Springfield, Missouri, hospital where he had been taken by ambulance following the shooting in Branson. Shortly before his death he told officers "he knew he was going to die" and his last statement was that a third brother, Fred, was innocent of bank robbery charges for which he was being tried in Larned, Kansas.

The FBI soon began replacing the Secret Service in investigating these types of cases and the Fleagle case became a famous new chapter among the annals of Colorado crime fighting.

Another robbery took place a little more than nine years later on a warm July day in 1937 when two men pulled up in front of the Minnequa Bank of Pueblo, got out, and entered the bank. They left eighteen minutes later $39,000 richer than when they went in.

A gold dental crown, a wooden leg, and a profane phrase all were to play their telltale parts in aiding agents of the FBI to solve one of the biggest bank robberies in Colorado's criminal history at that time.

Witnesses to the holdup remembered the leader of the group repeatedly uttered two profane words to his dapper partner as he exhorted him to hurry in collecting the money. Two passersby on the street recalled one of the bandits had to "brace himself with both hands" as he pulled his right foot into the car without stepping on the running board.

Not quite a year later one of the robbery suspects, William O. Bashaw, was killed when an airplane he was piloting crashed near Worland, Wyoming. Just a few months later his partner in crime, Henry A. Howard, who operated under a number of aliases, was arrested in Seattle. Coincidentally charges were filed against him in Denver the same day. Under questioning Howard frequently used the telltale profane words when he became agitated, and when witnesses were shown his picture, they identified him as the suspect in the robbery. While in custody, it was discovered he had a wooden leg due to a lumber camp accident fifteen years prior, which accounted for witnesses' description of him appearing to brace himself when getting into the getaway car.

A clear connection had been established between Howard and Bashaw. While arrangements were being made to exhume Bashaw's body to check for the gold-capped tooth, the FBI located the dentist who had replaced the gold tooth with a porcelain tooth soon after the robbery. The dentist produced a dental chart showing a gold pivot tooth as noted by victims of the robbery.

Howard, unable to post bail, was kept in the Denver County Jail after his arraignment in U. S. District Court in Denver in January 1939. He pleaded innocent to the robbery.

The FBI was busy following another connection between Howard and the third suspect and getaway driver, Robert Cline, who was serving a life sentence for armed robbery in Kentucky. The two had become acquainted while serving time in San Quentin Penitentiary for California robberies. When confronted with the information that the FBI had been talking with Robert Cline, Howard admitted to the Minnequa Bank robbery in addition to a recent post office holdup in Birmingham, Alabama. Howard was arraigned again and entered a guilty plea. He was sentenced to nine years in the federal penitentiary and moved to a branch of the California State Penitentiary in Represa to serve out the remainder of his San Quentin term.

This closed the FBI's files on the Minnequa Bank robbery and brought to an end the "prosperous days" in the late 1930s of the trio responsible for robberies throughout the country.

Newspaper clipping of Roy and Ruth Barnes shortly before Ruth Barnes was found guilty on contempt of court charges. After court was dismissed, Roy Barnes slugged me in the hallway outside U.S. District Court in Denver in 1947. (Rocky Mountain News Photo)

Chapter Fourteen

A COUPLE OF FELLAS NAMED ROY

IN EARLY 1947, I WAS COVERING A COURT PROCEEDING where a jury member, Ruth Barnes, was charged with contempt for answering questions while under oath that were partially false and withholding other information showing she was a biased jury member. She was found guilty and fined $100 as a sequel to her jury service in a case of a Denver auto dealer who was charged with violating odometer ceiling settings. Ruth Barnes had failed to reveal that the used car dealer and area rancher was her husband.

As I was leaving the court to file my story, Mr. Barnes punched me in the jaw because he felt I was sneering at him as I was taking notes. Although I had no recollection of even looking in his direction, I did return the hand of introduction.

A $100 fine was levied on Mr. Barnes for disrupting and disturbing court business. He also was relieved of $2,500 in civil court for assaulting me. I later heard he was attempting the same kind of persuasive instruction on one of his horses at his ranch when it kicked him, killing him instantly. That was one horse I never brought charges against.

By the end of the year, I had started a six-month investigative internship under the supervision of Ray Humphries, chief investigator for the Denver District Attorney's office. This job included working simultaneously as a special deputy to District Attorney John "Stump" Witcher of Cañon City.

As a reporter, I had often covered Warden Roy Best's administration in which he played fast and furious with state property. Best owned a ranch called the Hitchrack adjoining a privately-owned ranch frequently used by the Colorado State Penitentiary. One investigation I worked on uncovered co-mingling of the warden's private expenses with those of the state penitentiary. This included use of convict labor and the prison's heavy equipment and shipments of grass seed and livestock that belonged to the prison sent to the warden's ranch near Salida.

While these transactions could not be admitted as evidence in the trial because the witnesses could not prove that the items were taken from prison supplies, they were admissible in a civil service hearing because prison employees and inmates were involved.

During the investigation, personal expenditures made in the name of the Colorado State Penitentiary by Warden Best and his wife also came to light. They included car repairs for the warden's family members; various furniture and glassware purchased from Daniels & Fisher; chinaware, glassware, specialty silverware and silver service accessories purchased from Carson Crockery and delivered to the warden's home; and expensive clothing purchased by the warden from Neusteters, a high-end Denver department store, in the name of the Denver Pie Company account. These were personal purchases made from businesses with no viable dealings with the Colorado State Penitentiary and further evidence of improper charges to the state.

A report by Jack H. Gilmore for the state attorney general showed the state had paid unconscionable prices to the Colorado State Penitentiary for musical instruments, and furthermore, far more instruments were paid for than were accounted for in an audit. It became increasingly clear there had been a conspiracy to cheat and defraud the State of Colorado.

Testimony from nine inmates and one guard corroborated information about some prison records, which had been reported as accidentally burned but actually were burned on instructions from prison officials.

In addition, inmates and employees testified to a grand jury about unnecessary brutality at the prison. A letter and report passed along to the investigative team from a former chaplain at the penitentiary detailed some of the brutality and outlined what he viewed as "deeply entrenched faults of Colorado's penal system," which overshadowed twenty years of investigations, charges, counter charges, and personalities but resulted in nothing ever changing.

While grand jury indictments were being dropped, the civil rights and civil service case evidence was mounting. Fremont County DA Stump

Witcher outlined the evidence I had helped gather and informed Governor Dan Thornton of our findings. These revealed that some of the matters, while not criminal, detailed a lack of competency on the part of Warden Best.

Over the course of the next two and a half years, Warden Roy Best would be investigated by local, state, and federal officials and be tried and acquitted by a grand jury with the civil service charges seemingly abandoned.

However, on July 16, 1951, everything changed for the warden when a riot broke out at the Cañon City Penitentiary. The riot was subdued, but it became known that he had ordered the convicts involved be flogged. This was routine procedure for infractions and had been going on for years, as the chaplain had stated in his report.

In August, Roy Best suffered a heart attack and was in critical condition. However, in a month's time, he told the governor he would be back

Warden Roy Best (center) confers with his attorney, Anthony F. Zarlengo, as attorney Frederick E. Dickerson addresses the court, January 23, 1951. (Denver Post. Karol Smith of Cañon City, photographer.)

on the job. In October he was elected national president of the Wardens Association of the Congress of Corrections at a conference in Biloxi, Mississippi.

Time, however, was not on the warden's side. In mid-December I was sent to Washington, D.C., to present evidence of civil rights violations to the FBI, and as a result, they opened a secret probe into the floggings. Pressure on the governor and other state officials to oust the warden was mounting daily.

On March 25, 1952, Ben Brooks arrived from Washington to present the civil rights case to a federal grand jury. By the end of April, the grand jury indicted the warden and eight others for violating the civil rights of six convicts. It was revealed for the first time that charges had never been filed against the five convicts who instigated the riot.

A new U. S. District Judge, Delmas C. Hill, was appointed to try the civil rights case because District Judge W. Lee Knous disqualified himself. This was most fortunate since this case had been under investigation for so long. The court was routinely more than two years behind in its docket, resulting in litigants waiting many months before having their cases decided.

The civil service portion of the case ended up in the hands of S. T. Anderson, who was serving as special prosecutor in the Best case. Anderson was a superb trial lawyer. The warden and eight others pled not guilty and their attorneys asked for dismissal of the indictments, which was refused by the judge.

Warden Best refused to leave the job and give up his home. However, by the end of May with ouster charges filed by Governor Thornton and under suspension by the Board of Institutions, Warden Best vacated his house and moved back to his ranch near Salida.

The civil rights trial began in June 1952. In the trial, Best could not justify the use of violence on inmates in the state penitentiary. When the verdict was read, the defendant expressed displeasure at the outcome by threatening to have me meet with a bad accident. Fortunately the accident never came. Warden Best subsequently resigned his position as warden and an entirely new administrative team came in to manage the prison.

Chapter Fifteen

THE IN-BETWEEN YEARS

For the next three years, as my investigative internship with the Denver District Attorney's office came to a close, I traveled many different paths, often simultaneously. Those years would be some of my most interesting and personally rewarding.

I had decided to enroll in law school at Denver University's Westminster College of Law, but prior to entering law school in the fall of 1948, I joined the *Denver Post* in July as the night city editor covering the rewrite battery, which consisted of rewriting and polishing stories filed by reporters. I also covered the city desks and did some investigative reporting, and by 1951, I was tri-county editor.

Just as in a lawyer's life, life on a newspaper reporter's beat holds lessons of all kinds and yields stories funny, sad, and sometimes both. Some stories you never forget. One that comes to mind involved a pulverizing plant where anything could be pulverized. The plant had a fire and explosion one time, many times actually, and I was working on interviewing people afterward. I remember talking to the manager there. What I didn't realize then, was that he was in shock and waiting for the police and ambulance to come and haul him away. He was walking around rubbing his hands not making very much sense, and I was trying to interview him on how it feels to get blown out of a building.

One of the first breaking news events I dealt with at the *Post* was a most amazing vehicle collision when the Elitch Garden Amusement Park train derailed, scattering more than two dozen riders onto the rail siding. The paper couldn't find enough ambulances for all the injured people. Most of the more seriously injured had been thrown onto the siding.

Another interesting case involved Colonel Philip S. Van Cise, a distinguished Denver district attorney from 1921 to 1925, who had gone into private practice. Van Cise was best known for the arrest and prosecution of Lou Blonger, the leader of a million-dollar bunko ring that controlled the streets of Denver for more than twenty-five years. In his book, *Fighting the Underworld*, Van Cise detailed this period in Denver's crime fighting history.

Van Cise had a client who wanted divorce papers served on her husband who was just back from military service. As the man was receiving the news, which he took quite hard, it became clear to him his house was going to be taken away from him.

He also grew quite upset over the fact that Van Cise was representing his wife and got off a couple of shots at him. Fortunately, Van Cise was able to get out from behind his desk and grab the man's arm and hold it up in the air as he fired several more bullets into the ceiling.

Jack Frank, a fellow reporter at the *Denver Post*, and I responded to the ruckus. The police had already arrived, disarmed the man, and taken him into custody. Meanwhile, Van Cise was in a corner of his office emptying urine out of his shoe into a wastebasket.

Van Cise served as an attorney for the *Rocky Mountain News* for more than twenty years after leaving the district attorney's office. One of his more famous cases was defending the newspaper for libel when it was sued by *Denver Post* publisher Frederick Bonfils. The case never went to trial because Bonfils died.

I lost track of the number of shootings I covered. However, they were not as spectacular as the fires. All in all, it was a most exciting period of my life, and I wouldn't have traded it for anything.

Chapter Sixteen

RUTH GILLESPIE

DURING MY YEARS AT THE *DENVER POST* and while in law school, I had joined a local organization in Denver called the Young Republicans and soon became the chairman of the Colorado state delegation. A young woman by the name of Ruth Gillespie was a fellow member of the group, and she was the Colorado National Committeewoman delegate.

At about the same time, I was the editor of *The Colorado Republican*, a small weekly publication. Although no official affiliation existed between the weekly and the Young Republicans, it came to serve as our bully pulpit. Ruth was the associate editor of the paper, and our paths frequently crossed as a result. We soon discovered that we both found great pleasure in the newspaper work and in each other's company. Although the paper was not a profitable enterprise, it was a labor of love.

Ruth was born February 28, 1924, to Dean Milton Gillespie and Lillie May (Baldwin) Gillespie in Denver's Mercy Hospital. Coincidentally, I was born in the same hospital. Ruth's mother was a Pueblo, Colorado native, graduating in 1903 from Pueblo Centennial High School. Her father, Dean Gillespie, was born May 3, 1884, in Salina, Kansas, to a pioneer physician. Ruth's parents had another daughter, Jeanne, fourteen years older than Ruth and married to an attorney who practiced law in New York City. Ruth had attended East High School and upon graduation went on to study pre-law at the University of Colorado in Boulder.

In 1905 Ruth's father came to Denver. Within five years he would be married, have a daughter, and head his own truck and machinery distributing business, the White Truck Company. In October 1919 he was awarded

Ruth and me attending a Young Republicans gathering.

Ruth's father, Dean Gillespie, in his office at the White Truck Company in Denver.

a patent for his design of a specialized truck body that provided a lighter weight chassis, making it easily adaptable for carrying large construction material as well as general merchandise, thus decreasing construction costs. In 1920 he purchased the old Denver Omnibus & Cab Company building, located between Pearl and Washington Streets, and moved his distributing company to this location.

Ruth, meanwhile, was pursuing a law degree at Columbia University in New York. Law school in the 1940s presented some significant challenges for Ruth. She was a young woman at a time when most law schools had few female law students, but her passion for the law saw her through. She found it very interesting and loved the practice of law. She returned to Denver to become one of Colorado's first female attorneys, practicing with the Dayton Denious law firm, where she specialized in tax law for ten years.

During a special election held in the First District of Colorado to fill the vacancy caused by the death of the Honorable Lawrence Lewis, Dean

The White Scout Truck parked in front of the White Truck Company in Denver.

Gillespie was elected to the U.S. House of Representatives in March 1944. He was re-elected to the Seventy-ninth Congress for the 1944-1946 term of office. He served on the Appropriations Committee and traveled the world in this capacity. He found politics fascinating and adored being in the House.

Ruth was very close to her father and helped him with many of his business projects. She served as his campaign manager when he ran for re-election in 1946 to his seat in the U.S. House of Representatives. He was defeated and returned to private business in Denver until his death three years later. Dean Gillespie's service as a member of Congress came late in life for him, which was too bad because he enjoyed it immensely.

Ruth's involvement in his campaigns likely sparked her interest in politics. My mother was a Republican committeewoman, and from the earliest times, I was dabbling in politics. I'm sure Ruth dabbled in politics from a young age, too.

At his death on February 2, 1949, Ruth's father was president of Dean Gillespie & Company; vice president and treasurer of Bluehill Foods

Dean Gillespie in his personal car with his driver.

Corporation of Denver; and president of Motoroyal Oil Company, Denver. Over the course of his business career, he had headed up twenty-four separate corporations. He was also a member of the Denver Rotary, Denver Athletic Club, Society of Automotive Engineers, Society for Research of Meteorites, and Society of American Military Engineers. In addition, he belonged to the Elks, the Masons, and was a Shriner. He was considered one of the outstanding business and political leaders of the State of Colorado with business interests throughout Colorado and Wyoming.

On February 3, 1949, many memorial messages were entered into the *Congressional Record* by Dean Gillespie's friends and colleagues in Congress who held him in high regard and deeply respected him for his business acumen as well as his unique Western convictions and perspective. He had been one of the very few people still living who knew of conditions in the early days of the West.

One of his great hobbies and passions was collecting meteorites. As a small boy, Dean became interested in what he called falling stars as he drove the horse and buggy for his father, a pioneer country doctor. He

Specialized construction trucks, with the patented chassis designed by Dean Gillespie, being loaded with sand and gravel.

would watch the night skies on his father's rounds as he made house calls. As an adult he traveled in the West and took every opportunity to investigate reported meteorite falls. He frequently spoke on the subject and became nationally known for his interest.

Dean's meteorite collection was one of the world's largest private collections and included 192 individual pieces representing 17 distinct meteorite falls. The majority, 136 samples in all, were heavy "irons" collected from the meteorite crater of the Arizona Cañon Diablo area and collectively weighing more than one ton. Eleven were classified as aerolites or "stony" meteorites. After her father's death Ruth donated his collection to the Denver Museum of Natural History, now the Denver Museum of Nature and Science.

Law school and my work at the *Post* continued to dominate my days and nights. Ruth was practicing law while simultaneously managing her father's properties and settling his estate.

One of the things I enjoyed most about being in the newspaper business was the chance to meet and be with famous people and learn their life stories. One of those interesting people was Erle Stanley Gardner, lawyer

The White model 15 (1500 lb.) modern "chuck wagon" doing service on the roadless prairie of the C. J. Belden ranch in Pitchfork, Wyoming.

and author best known for the detective series featuring Perry Mason. Our acquaintance dated back to 1949 when he and Dr. Lemoyne Snyder came to Denver to work on the Joe Sam Walker murder case in Boulder. Walker was tried and later convicted in November 1948 of the murder of Theresa Foster, a Greeley-area farm girl who was a CU coed.

The case broke on November 11 when the girl's body was found under a bridge on the Old Stage Road outside of Boulder. She had been thrown from atop the bridge and subsequently died from loss of blood and shock from her injuries.

Snyder was a lawyer, medical doctor, and pathologist who had been a medical legal expert for the Michigan State Police. Gardner and he were just completing participation in a court of last resort on a major murder case in Bermuda under the sponsorship of a monthly magazine. Gardner was a bear of a man who practiced law for more than twenty-two years. He spoke fluent Chinese and was highly regarded by the California Chinese community whom he represented in a number of legal matters.

He and Dr. Snyder responded to a call for help from the *Denver Post*. As a reporter at the *Post*, I was well aware the newspaper had been frustrated with the lack of progress in solving the murder. A small army of newspaper reporters had been assigned to the story and an alerted general public turned out in the hundreds to search vacant fields for evidence and clues.

As time passed, all eyes began to focus on Joe Sam Walker, a sheet metal worker who lived in Eldorado Springs. It was thought he enticed Theresa Foster into his car as she left a meeting on campus one cold night.

There appeared to have been a massive fight in the car during which Theresa hit her assailant on the head with a wrench. In turn, she sustained many injuries and later, unconscious and bleeding, the murderer allegedly threw her off a bridge on the Old Stage Road. Her body was found in a ravine near a bridge south of Boulder on the Boulder-Golden highway. That was my introduction to the case on Armistice Day, 1948.

During the course of a two-week period, I drove more than 2,000 miles with Gardner, Snyder, and Post city editor Gene Lowell. My job was to supervise coverage of the story and personally check out many leads. Each evening we would head back to Denver where Gardner and Snyder were staying at the Brown Palace Hotel. The next day we would have breakfast at the hotel and head back to Boulder.

Two homicide detectives from Denver, James O'Donnell and Joe Holindrake, were assigned to the case. In the 1940s the Denver Police Department tried to assist the smaller sheriffs' offices and police departments in all major homicides, so this was not unusual. However, Boulder County Sheriff Art Everson was getting more assistance than he really wanted in this case.

A couple of items were significant. Walker had painted the inside of his car red immediately after the attack to mask any blood stains, and he had developed a severe infection in his head wounds. Eventually, Joe Sam Walker was arrested. At one point he almost admitted the murder, but his story was that he had gotten into a fight with a blond youth after picking up the Foster woman, and he stuck with that to the end. Since there were no eyewitnesses, the death penalty was out of the question.

At the close of his trial, District Judge George Bradfield sentenced Walker to eighty years to life. This was a significant sentence at that time. Some lawyers in Denver felt the sentence reflected overly heavy coverage of the investigation and arrest in the newspapers, particularly the *Denver Post.*

Against this fully packed schedule, Ruth and I were trying to get married, but every time we set a date for our wedding, the Walker trial date would be moved. When we finally managed to squeeze in an evening wedding ceremony on April 22, 1949, it was a photo finish. We had a very few hours for a brief, one-night honeymoon at the Broadmoor Hotel in Colorado Springs. Then I was off for two weeks to cover the trial in Boulder, and Ruth returned to her law practice in Denver.

Those were two weeks of rare excitement in meeting and working with America's unforgettable author of crime stories. For millions of readers, the fictional attorney Perry Mason and his secretary Della Street will forever live in their memories. Gardner always felt that Hollywood did not fully appreciate the characters he was trying to portray as Perry Mason and Della Street. He felt they set aside his concerns and gave his stories the Hollywood touch.

Walker served twenty years in prison, but maintained his innocence throughout his trial and imprisonment. In 1969 the high court overturned his conviction based on evidence presented surrounding the extraordinary pretrial publicity.

The judge ordered Walker be given a new trial within fifteen days or be set free. Boulder County District Attorney Stanley Johnson determined not to retry the 20-year-old case and Joe Sam Walker was set free in August 1969.

In 1983 a story moved on the Associated Press teletype that Joe Sam Walker had committed suicide in a Texas motel. I called retired special prosecutor Hatfield Chilson of Loveland and he commented, "Well, I guess when we got through, he gave himself the death sentence."

This was the front-page headline in the Rocky Mountain News *on August 16, 1946, describing the clampdown on gambling spots in Idaho Springs, an old mining town in the mountains west of Denver.*

Chapter Seventeen

NARROW ESCAPE IN IDAHO SPRINGS

A RATHER SCARY EVENT TOOK PLACE ONE EVENING when fellow reporter Bill Wood and I drove to Idaho Springs. We had been working on a series of articles surrounding the Smaldones, a Denver family with many business interests, some of which included gambling. These articles had shed light into some dark areas of gambling in Denver and surrounding small towns. Our articles had effectively shut down many of the Smaldones' establishments.

Bill was determined to report on a run-in with some of the gamblers. He claimed they had started a fight with him the night before, but I was skeptical. Since I had a car, Bill persuaded me to drive him to Idaho Springs to a particular restaurant. As I was paying the dinner bill and preparing to leave, Lea Shaducks, a Denver bondswoman and a good friend, took me by the arm and told me to be very careful leaving the restaurant and especially walking to my car. As I thanked her for the advice, she said goodbye, again reiterating I should "take care of myself."

Unnerving as this was, Bill and I managed to make it to the car all right, but as we started down the winding canyon road from Idaho Springs to Denver I noticed that the car wasn't operating as well as it had coming up. It became more obvious with each curve that it had been tampered with while we were in the restaurant.

We were heavily armed. I had my father-in-law's old hunting rifle in the car, and it was a canon. Bill and I each had side arms. I'm not sure we would have known what to do with them, but we had them. I had taken marksmanship training in military school and was a fair shot but was completely untested under this type of circumstance.

The more worrying matter was we had a car full of thugs in hot pursuit and we couldn't attract the attention of the State Highway Patrol. My car was not equipped with a two-way radio and there weren't any officers out patrolling, so the only thing to do was glide down Coal Creek Canyon into Golden.

On the last downhill slope coming into the foothills of Golden, I swerved into a service station. We quickly pulled the car into the garage and jacked it up while the owner turned out the station lights. With the car now quite literally out of commission, there was nothing to do but abandon it and hike up the side of the adjacent hill. In the dark, just as we came to the crest of the hill, we turned and looked down toward the road and watched as the pursuing car raced past, never slowing, with only moments to spare. Upon reflection I came to the realization that at times of great fear and stress it is startling how quickly actions unfold and how swiftly human beings can accomplish things they would never believe themselves capable of under normal circumstances.

With great relief we made our way back down the hillside and called the Highway Patrol from the gas station. A division captain came to pick us up in his patrol car. About the time our pursuers realized they had lost us, we were riding in a patrol car with a man at the wheel who had the most incredible eyesight. He could see cars ahead of us that I sure couldn't see.

Bill and I met at the city editor's house that night to make plans for the next article in our series. Remarkably, the next day the Post received an apology from the Smaldones for their "boys getting a little overzealous."

Chapter Eighteen

YEARS IN DENVER DISTRICT ATTORNEY OFFICE

IN JANUARY 1952, I WAS APPOINTED DEPUTY DISTRICT ATTORNEY in the Denver DA's office. To say this was an extremely busy time would be a huge understatement, but I seemed to thrive on the work. We were located in the old West Side Court building on West Colfax, adjoining the Denver County Jail.

In addition to the District Attorney, we had around fourteen deputies and many others assisting. Among these was Ellett M. Shepherd, who was the complaint deputy. He spent his time meeting with police officers and determining which cases to file. All these cases then were filed by the District Attorney in the court and thus began the process through the system for trial.

There was also Max D. Melville who was the assistant district attorney and a brilliant lawyer. He spent much of his time writing monologues on the Supreme Court findings and advising the district attorney on cases. Frederick E. Dickerson was considered one of the ablest district attorneys and was a most distinguished jurist. He later had a defense attorney associate by the name of Anthony F. Zarlengo, a former deputy district attorney himself.

The deputies were divided into two groups, and my partner, Jim Flanigan, was a veteran of many cases. Ultimately, he was named a District Judge, and a beautiful courthouse was built in his honor, now known as the Lindsey-Flanigan Courthouse.

I saw the law and journalism as closely tied. There is a great similarity between the two. Both involve writing, interviewing, and a tremendous amount of preparation, especially in trial law. You work with so many people.

Everyone used to joke that when the murder cases were assigned, Jim and I got double the share of filings. For some reason our division kept getting the murder cases. I tried nine murder cases during my years with the DA's office. It was a matter of just getting in there and doing a kind of newspaper job of interviewing, gathering facts and details, and asking lots of questions. Gradually it would all come together. I never liked to try cases where I had not done a thorough job of interviewing, so usually I would talk with witnesses and review their cases and testimony. This gave me quite a lot to do each night after a busy day in trial.

We had to start every case by picking the twelve members of the jury. This was a great experience in itself because many of these people had served as jurors in previous cases and often they knew as much about the case and the trial routine as we did.

It became apparent in many cases that while we had substantial authority, the case fell far short of how it would have been handled on TV. We had to explain to the jurors that this was not a TV case but the real thing.

One case always bothered me. I failed to prove the crime had occurred in the City and County of Denver, and Judge Francis E. Hickey dismissed the case. He refused to let me reopen the case for new evidence, and the defendant walked out a free man. I sought not to make mistakes of that nature again.

We maintained a steady briefing of new state and Supreme Court trial proceedings, which was an ongoing education in itself. I easily saw why they considered a term in the DA's office the finest legal experience one could get. If we failed to get convictions, the police often would consider us unsatisfactory triers of fact. I participated in prosecution of 35 jury trials with 35 resulting in convictions. The police liked that. Many of our opponents were represented by former trial deputies, and in several cases, they were far more experienced.

Jim and I took turns presiding over routine cases, and we often swore our jurors over dead bodies in the coroner's office. This was following the age-old ritual of conducting inquests into wrongful deaths. We didn't get any particular complaints from the deceased, although there were a few times I thought we might.

In one murder case I prosecuted, a wrongful death almost took place in the courtroom. Irving Andrew was the defense attorney and a very tall

A copy of The Case of the Fugitive Nurse *by Erle Stanley Gardner was inscribed and given to me by Gardner in thanks for some law research I did for him.*

man. The trial was fairly straightforward, and the jury found the defendant guilty. However, as the court clerk read the findings of the jury, she misread one count stating the death penalty had been called for, which so shocked Mr. Andrew that he fainted, falling to the floor with quite a thud. The police ambulance was called, and I rode with him to the hospital. The defendant and the defense attorney spent a number of anguishing hours before the true verdict was cleared up.

Another case I distinctly remember involved a local gambler, Fats Falbo, whose body was found in a bullet-riddled car that certainly spoiled his very nice clothes. He and Murph Cohen, another local gambler, had managed to eat a spoonful of Italian salad just prior to being taken for a ride. Fats Falbo was found sitting in his car looking up from his location at the bottom of a big lake. Murph Cohen was attached to a rail section and placed in the water as well. Although I did not personally work on the case, I believed the two murders resulted from the victims being deeply in debt to the Mafia and having trouble paying off their debts.

My friend and ex-boss Ray Humphreys used to reel off names of murder victims many of whom I thought must be cousins. These slayings occurred in and around Denver during the Prohibition Era of the 1920s clear up through the 1950s. Many of the slayings were thought to be the handiwork of the Mafia, but could never be proven so there were never any convictions. I grew up around many of the stories of the short, remarkable lives of some of these people.

At the time I did not realize both Ray Humphreys and Earl Wettengel, the former district attorney, had received death threats, so not all of the dangerous criminals were given sudden death, such as was the case in the Fats Falbo case. I took a lesson from cases such as these and did not start up my car without first checking under the hood for foreign objects buried there.

By the early 1950s, Erle Stanley Gardner had made Denver his home and was writing more Perry Mason books. On one occasion, he came to me for assistance pertaining to specific Colorado laws, which were different from what he had referenced in many of his other books. Gardner inscribed my copy of the book titled *The Case of the Fugitive Nurse*, "To Ed Lehman, who assisted in writing this book by digging up the low down on the Colorado law. With all my thanks, Erle Stanley Gardner, January 1954"

Chapter Nineteen

THE DOODLEBUG CASE

ONE OF THE STRANGEST AND MOST UNUSUAL CASES I was involved in came to the DA's office by way of *San Francisco Chronicle* reporter J. P. Cahn. It would come to be known as the Doodlebug case. The incredible story started long before it ever got to the Denver courtroom in 1952, where I was the assistant prosecuting attorney to Bert Keating, who was the chief trial lawyer in the case.

It all began in 1948, near Aztec, New Mexico, with the crash of a dome-shaped aircraft, seemingly not of human origin. The military quickly recovered the craft and everything in it.

In 1950 a Hollywood writer named Frank Scully published a book titled, *Behind the Flying Saucers*. In it he reported there had been a number of small, humanoid alien bodies recovered from the Aztec crash site. Mr. Scully's sources for many of the claims in his book were two men, Leo GeBauer and Silas M. Newton, who were oil investors and speculators with business dealings in Arizona, Colorado, New Mexico, and Utah. They supposedly met each other while working a con on Denver industrialist millionaire Herman Flader.

GeBauer had been a government maintenance engineer when, upon leaving the service, he had a chance to buy an electric box with magnetic properties. He touted this device as capable of finding oil or gold.

In August 1949, GeBauer and Newton were driving through the Mojave Desert when they heard about the crash in Aztec. The con that came to be known as the Doodlebug case was hatched.

GeBauer had a plant in Arizona where he maintained shop equipment. In Scully's book, GeBauer was thinly disguised as a mysterious government scientist, identified as "Dr. Gee", although GeBauer always denied he was Dr. Gee. Newton, a noted golfer, was the pitchman. He made a lot of his investor contacts on the golf course. He would ply likely investors with details of the recent crash of the alien craft and analysis by top-secret government labs of the discovery of magnetic devices that could locate oil or gold. He advised these investors that he could get them access to this "alien" technology for an exchange of money. Once they agreed, details of the required investment would quickly be drawn up.

Newton had convinced Scully to write the book about the Aztec crash in the first place. Scully apparently was conned as well because he wrote everything just as Newton and GeBauer told it to him—hook, line, and sinker. The book gave these two con men considerable free publicity and some degree of believability and trustworthiness, but it would not last.

The scheme was to pretend they had located underground oil. There was a particular site in California where the Pacific Gas and Electric Company held the license agreements. GeBauer and Newton pitched the property to Herman Flader as likely to contain oil. Newton and GeBauer took him out to the property and turned on "the Doodlebug" to do its performance, that is, to signal there was oil underground.

Along came J. P. Cahn, reporter with the *San Francisco Chronicle*. While talking one day with Newton, he succeeded in swapping out a small piece of the so-called alien ship with another piece of metal. When he had the alien metal tested, it turned out to be of human origin—the same grade of aluminum used for pots and pans.

At the subsequent trial, one of our principle witnesses was a land agent for PG & E. He said the area where they were looking was known as "cemetery marble" by local geologists. GeBauer and Newton proposed to drill deeply in response to the purported radiation signals from the Doodlebug. Herman Flader's main role was to bring his checkbook and write checks whenever Newton and GeBauer needed money.

I was becoming aware of a steady stream of revolving FBI agents in Denver, California, and at the proposed drilling site, which led me to believe J. P. Cahn was keeping them informed of his findings and suspicions. Their boss, J. Edgar Hoover, was also quite interested in the case as it involved government property. Aircraft made of aluminum was new technology at this time. Any accidents were investigated by the military and the FBI with all remnants immediately being collected for further investigation.

Once Cahn's findings were published in 1952, several fraud victims came forward to tell about their dealings with Newton and GeBauer. Unfortunately they had no recourse to press charges against the two men due to the statute of limitations. However, Denver millionaire Herman Flader did not fall into this category as he had a solid case. Newton and GeBauer were arrested by the FBI and went to trial in November 1953.

It was rumored the government purchased caskets for the dozen or so "little people" who were in the doomed craft, so we couldn't call any of them as witnesses. Bert Keating got so mad about this—he felt we were trying a case against midgets.

I worked with Flader on weekends preparing him to testify. He often told me he believed that anything was possible. With that kind of open-minded approach, he listened to Newton and GeBauer, which led to them receiving a number of checks from him to invest in a presumed rich oil-field in California.

Ike Mellman and his son, John, were the co-defense attorneys and very experienced trial lawyers, who usually won their cases on appeal. I remember Ike was obsessively concerned about us opening up the Doodlebug. Ike warned us it would blow up into many pieces and wanted us to keep our hands off so we wouldn't be injured in the explosion. He didn't want to be around when we began tampering with it, but we weren't too worried because we had the Doodlebug X-rayed and dissected in a lab. It never blew up.

During the trial, an interesting detail came out when an $18,500 "tuner" used by the con men turned out to be indistinguishable from a matching item found in a local hardware store for $3.50. In the end, GeBauer and Newton were quickly convicted and ordered to pay $18,000 in damages to Herman Flader. Thus was the outcome of the Doodlebug case, which was also my last case with the Denver District Attorney's office.

Me during my two-year term in the Colorado State Legislature. I was elected from Denver.

Chapter Twenty

COLORADO STATE LEGISLATURE

IN 1954 I WAS ELECTED from the first district in Denver to one, two-year term in the state legislature, serving as a member of the Education, Interstate Cooperation, and Judiciary Committees. I was assigned then-Governor Ed Johnson's former desk in the state legislature. He did well by the seat during his term, so I figured I should as well.

By 1955 I had been appointed to three subcommittees—Civil Defense, Crime Correction & Control, and Legislative Processes & Procedures, which was chaired by Rep. William O. Lennox.

I was asked to lead a joint effort between Colorado and Utah to obtain an Interstate Highway System designation for a Denver to Salt Lake City route. Harry S. Allen of the Legislative Council and I met in Salt Lake City with Utah legislative and Chamber of Commerce officials. This group included: Clair Hopkins, Utah House majority leader, from Vernal; Lewis H. Lloyd, Director of the Legislative Council at the state capitol; L. Y. Sidnay, Executive Director of the Vernal Chamber of Commerce; Dilworth Woolley, Utah Senator and head of the Senate Highway Committee at the state capitol; Weston E. Hamilton, Executive Director of the Salt Lake City Chamber of Commerce; Merrill K. Davis, Utah State Senator; Miles P. Romney, Manager Utah Mining Association in Salt Lake City; and Jay Smith, from Mountain States Telephone & Telegraph.

In late February 1955, I addressed the Utah House of Representatives, which was one of my first experiences with public speaking other than courtroom presentations, and to my surprise found that I thoroughly enjoyed it. I met with the Utah Senate Highway Commission where leaders of both houses made assurances of Utah's resolution to Congress regarding the route. It also was agreed that Lewis Lloyd, head of the Utah Legislative Council, would accept the assignment to follow through on the proposed highway extension, even though the final decision was many years distant.

The Utah conference also determined that the Interstate Cooperation Commissions of the two states would closely follow developments and integrate their work with the State Highway Commissions of the respective states. Utah authorities gave their assurances that a resolution could be passed and transmitted to Washington, D.C., before the Utah legislature ended its session on March 10, 1955. Thus was the first meeting of cooperation between Colorado and Utah. Many other studies would follow to determine the best route for what would become Interstate 70 through the Colorado Rocky Mountains and west through Utah.

The Federal-Aid Highway Act was immensely helpful in preventing this huge project from languishing on the drawing boards. The act, which was signed in 1956 by President Dwight Eisenhower, began the interstate highway system throughout the country and made federal funds available through the Interstate Commerce Committee.

Several on-site inspections of proposed locations for a highway toll tunnel through the Continental Divide were made in the spring of 1956. One study was the Berthoud Pass tunnel site. This was the precursor to what finally became the present-day Eisenhower Tunnel, linking the eastern side of the Continental Divide with the Western Slope through Glenwood Canyon. I worked with a group of Utah legislators who were confident there eventually would be a tunnel and requested that Colorado consider naming it after President Eisenhower, which I thought entirely appropriate. Today the tunnels are named the Eisenhower-Johnson Memorial Tunnels in remembrance of both the former president and former Colorado governor and U. S. Senator Edwin C. Johnson.

Whenever I travel this highway or see it on television, I can't help but recall all the time, effort, and cooperation required to get this massive but marvelous project started, let alone completed. I consider my contribution those many years ago to be the highlight of my public service in the state legislature.

Chapter Twenty-One

PRIVATE LAW PRACTICE

RUTH AND I OPENED OUR OWN LAW PRACTICE with partner Bill Burnett after I left the Denver District Attorney's office in 1954. Our specialties covered criminal, general, and tax law. Ruth loved the law and loved practicing it. She liked helping people. Law practice in those days was a lot different than it is today. It was an enriching personal experience. Lawyers then did not make as much money as lawyers today, but they got a great deal of satisfaction from what they were doing. Ruth was a good advocate and a very talented attorney, and she really wanted to practice law.

Dating back to our time together on *The Colorado Republican*, Ruth was aware that one of my aims in life was to purchase a small daily newspaper. Fortunately, she had printers ink coursing through her veins too. Newspapers had been part of her family background back a couple of generations when they published prohibition newspapers in Kansas. Prohibition newspapers were publications supporting Prohibition, which banned the transportation, sale, and manufacturing of alcoholic beverages.

By 1955 we were searching for a newspaper to buy, but finding the right newspaper for sale at the right price was the challenge. Oddly enough, practically all the major papers for sale were in the South as that region was facing tremendous racial upheaval. A lot of the old-timers there were deciding it was a great time to get out. I warned Ruth that a couple of Western Yankees in the South would be at quite a disadvantage and we probably would lose our advertising along with our front windows. So we turned our sights north.

Longmont had long appealed to me. As a child, Mother and I traveled by train to the area in the course of her real estate business. I always

In June 1953, Ruth and I and five-month-old Dean celebrated Ruthann's second birthday.

thought what an interesting community it was as I'd look out at the dirt streets. In later years, I was in the region quite a bit on assignments for the Denver Post and got to know the area even better.

I loved journalism, but Ruth was in love with the law, so I had to talk her out of practicing law. That was a tall order. She was a very good lawyer. As fortune would have it, she agreed to join me in the newspaper business, but she always maintained her ties to the practice of law. She remained a member of the Colorado and Boulder County Bar Associations throughout her newspaper career. Ruth later served on a panel on White House Fellowships from the Denver area, as legislative head of the Colorado Commission on the Status of Women, as a member of the judicial nominating committee for Colorado's 20th Judicial District, and as a member of the Colorado Supreme Court's Judicial Advisory Committee.

A doctor once told me it was a bad idea for a man to be in business with his wife. He was wrong, of course. His advice was one of the more ridiculous recommendations I've received during my life. Maybe he couldn't be in business with his wife, but for me it was a very good experience.

February 7, 1957. Ruth and I had just purchased the Times-Call *in Longmont.*

Another wonderful experience of a quite different nature occurred in June 1951 when Ruth and I welcomed a daughter into our lives. We named her Ruthann. She was followed two years later in January 1953 by a son we named Dean Gillespie Lehman, after Ruth's father. They immediately became a delight and joy to watch as they grew up. They enriched our lives and made us very proud as they became adults.

We started out with the thought that by moving to a smaller community we still could do some things with law, but it quickly became apparent the confidentiality required in a law practice conflicted substantially with the responsibility of newsgathering for the newspaper. We had been looking for about two years when we discovered several shareholders of the *Times-Call* in Longmont were interested in selling. We were about to embark on the high seas of the newspaper business. The deal was closed on February 1, 1957, and we moved the family to Longmont.

PART FOUR
The Publishing Years

Chapter Twenty-Two

OUR NEWSPAPER PUBLISHING ADVENTURE BEGINS

LONGMONT'S POPULATION WAS APPROXIMATELY 11,000, and the paper's circulation was 4,000. As with many newspapers in the West, what is now the *Longmont Daily Times-Call* had a varied history of publications and owners.

The first was the *Burlington Free Press* owned by the Beckwith brothers, Elmer and Fred. The articles on those crackling, fragile pages have a visionary foretelling feel. Education, water issues, politics, and government were the concerns of that day, just as they are now. In fact, the very first issue of the newspaper conveyed this regarding the hardships faced: "Any one who came on to St. Vrains, in the summer of 1860, and remained until the present time, and noted the changes, that have occurred since then; in the face of all the obstacles that the settlers have had to contend with, (including Indians and Grasshoppers) has reason to be thankful." (*Burlington Free Press*, April 26, 1871)

The May 5, 1871, edition carried this notice: "The tax payers of this School District will be glad to know the last Dollar, of the school house Debt is now paid, and enough taxes remain unpaid, to paint the school house, and fence the Lot."

In the same issue, the editor boasted confidently of the region's water supplies: "Will there be water enough, for us all, is the question, some of the new settlers are inclined to ask. We answer, Yes, there is. . . . We would say to them, go ahead with your ditches, and if you get enough of them built, in the next ten years, to drain St. Vrain in the summer, when the largest part of the irrigation is being done, we will give up beat, but not until then."

The young paper carried advertisements from the town's businesspeople and entrepreneurs. Businesses were so enthusiastic about having a newspaper in their midst that every one of them advertised in the first edition, according to author Dorothy Large in her book, *Old Burlington*.

The newspaper reflected the town it covered, but by 1872 nearly every business and household, including the newspaper, had packed up and moved up the hill to Longmont, then known as the Chicago-Colorado Colony. Burlington eventually faded into obscurity. Though short-lived—the *Burlington Free Press* consisted of only two issues—the publication marked the beginning of Elmer Beckwith's long newspaper career in Longmont.

The following year Elmer Beckwith changed the name of the paper three times—from the *Longmont Sentinel* to the *Colorado Press* to, finally, the *Longmont Press*—presumably to match the name of the town it now called home.

> *When members of the Chicago-Colorado Colony founded Longmont in 1871, they brought west not only their belongings, but also the firmly held values that guided their lives. The Colony motto, 'Industry, Morality and Temperance,' declared in no uncertain terms their commitment to righteousness and hard work; and the plat of their new town. . .dotted with lots reserved for churches, schools, a library and a university, reflected the importance they attached to both religion and education.*
> —Dale Bernard in the Longmont Daily Times-Call, October 1993

D. G. Scouten, formerly of the *Boulder News*, bought the *Longmont Press* in October 1872 with Beckwith remaining as publisher until 1885. In September 1879 a Main Street fire destroyed the *Longmont Press* building. Brothers L. H. Smith and Lowell S. Smith became the new owners in 1887 and were listed as the publishers. By 1888 they had changed the name to the *Longmont Times*, but by 1892 Beckwith had repurchased the paper with his sons E. Francis and Fenton S., and in 1893 it became a six-days-a-week paper with another new name of *Longmont Daily Times*. It was printed on a Proudy press, hand-cranked at first and later gas-powered. A steam-powered Cranston press would follow. In 1894 the Smith brothers were back again as editors/publishers. In 1895 Elmer Beckwith bought the paper one last time, filling the roles of owner/editor/publisher. It was the first newspaper in northern Colorado to install a Model 3

Linotype, which could set as much type in one hour as had previously taken a good compositor five hours to set.

Linotype operator Ray Lanyon purchased the Beckwith interest in the *Daily Times* in 1919. Lanyon had started in the business as a young boy delivering newspapers on foot in 1898. After a five-year printer's apprenticeship, he rose to the position of shop foreman. He served as publisher/owner in a career that would span fifty-nine years.

Competition arrived in 1897 when William Forgey, a former schoolteacher who had come to Colorado in 1886, launched a weekly, the *Saturday Evening Call*. A year later he sold the paper to George W. Johnson, former publisher of the *Berthoud Bulletin*, also owned by Forgey. Johnson had moved his family from Berthoud to Longmont in order to manage the Silver Moon Hotel at the corner of Third Avenue and Kimbark Street. He changed the name of the paper to the *Longmont Call* and published it on the second floor of the Charles Smith Drug Store at 372 Main Street.

In 1900, after acquiring additional equipment from a defunct newspaper in Ward—a mining town located in the foothills northwest of Boulder—Johnson moved the *Longmont Call* to 655 Fourth Avenue, adding a daily paper to the press run six years later. It remained in this location until 1964. Bernard "Bernie" Faller joined the *Longmont Call* as city editor and editorial writer in 1925. Johnson's two sons, Loren H. and Jean W., had become co-owners with their father by 1927, but George W. Johnson died in September 1929.

A local physician, Dr. J. A. Matlack, bought the *Longmont Call* in March 1905 from Mrs. Johnson and her two sons and renamed it the *Daily Call*. One of the sons, Jean W. Johnson, stayed on as city editor and business manager until 1965, when he suffered a fatal heart attack. Originally from Chester, Illinois, where he had published a newspaper before becoming a doctor, Matlack was on the staff at Longmont Hospital.

Longmont had built a hydropower plant in 1911 on the North St. Vrain River, providing reliable electric power to its residents. In 1912 the *Daily Times* took full advantage of this new power source and replaced its steam engine with an electric motor to drive the press. These improvements began what would become routine modernization well into the twenty-first century.

Otis Moore had started working for the *Daily Times* in 1905 as a 12-year-old newspaper carrier. When he left home at age 15, the paper's owner, Elmer Beckwith, let him sleep on a cot in the pressroom. Moore

The Colorado Press *occupied this building in Longmont in 1871 and 1872, after the community moved to Longmont from the Burlington site. Elmer Beckwith had published only two editions of the* Burlington Free Press *before it was suspended May 5, 1871. This frame building was on the southwest corner of 3rd Avenue and Main Street. It later was moved, and the basic structure today is a Longmont home.*

worked at the *Daily Times* as a printer until 1918, when he took a job with a Cheyenne, Wyoming, newspaper, but returned in 1919 as a printer when Lanyon took over the paper. Moore acquired a one-third interest in the paper in 1927, taking on the responsibilities of co-publisher until 1943.

The two competing newspapers—the *Daily Times* and the *Daily Call*—each with daily and weekly publications, merged on May 19, 1931, giving birth to the *Longmont Daily Times-Call*. Within a year, after acquiring Associated Press service, publication of the two weeklies ceased. A new flatbed, roll-fed press was installed at the Fourth Avenue location. With the move of the *Longmont Times'* operations, Lanyon became managing editor and co-owner. Matlack's son Jim was named associate editor, and Moore was named production superintendent. Faller

The Daily Times *building, 336-338 Main Street as it was rebuilt after a disastrous fire in 1879, which destroyed the newspaper plant. In 1931 the* Daily Times *moved from this plant to the enlarged building on Fourth Avenue when it merged with the* Longmont Call.

continued to serve as the newspaper's city editor. In 1943, Moore sold his one-third interest in the paper to Faller, who became partners with Matlack and Lanyon.

The line between news and editorial comment in those early-day newspapers was often blurred. The March 14, 1903, edition of the *Longmont Call* noted, under the headline "Sewers," "The need of sewers was never more apparent in Longmont than now." In the April 4, 1903, edition, the editor's attention turned to parking with this, "Hitching Posts. Very often there are days when there is not a vacant post to hitch to."

Pages of turn-of-the-century newspapers weren't devoted solely to news and opinion, however. Cautionary tales, often turning on twists of fate, were presented. There were fiction stories of love and mystery, jokes,

The Longmont Daily Times-Call *building from 1931 to 1964 at 655 Fourth Avenue as it appeared in the late 1940s. The* Daily Call *originally moved to this location in 1900 and occupied only a portion of the plant. A new press was installed when the newspapers consolidated on May 19, 1931. In 1970 the* Longmont Daily Times-Call *reoccupied the building as an annex to handle some of the first computer systems in phase one of moving from hot metal to cold type with electronic printing equipment.*

and household tips. Even cultural trends of the day were noted, such as a bulletin reprinted from the *Fort Collins Courier* in a 1904 edition of *The Call*, informing readers of the disappearance of the spoon holder from fashionable tables.

An essay by Faller's son, Bernard A. Faller Jr., described the elder Faller's deep love for covering the news in Longmont in the 1930s and 1940s. As a boy, the younger Faller was in awe of the *Times-Call* newsroom. His father granted him the occasional visit, provided he looked but did not speak. Questions were to be saved for discussion with his father later. It reveals not only a passion for the business, but a child's perspective on the sights, sounds, smells, and people of the newsroom of his father's day.

In its 93rd year (1964), the Longmont Daily Times-Call *moved to a new building at the corner of Fourth Avenue and Terry Street.*

A Love Affair with Words—
A Country Editor's Son Remembers
by Bernard A. Faller Jr.

In the background I could hear the old, flatbed press groaning and growling with a thumping sound occasionally. There was always concern, no, just plain unmitigated worry, that there'd be a web break, and it would be twilight before the carriers could mount their bikes, if even then.

It was truly magic. And the magic put a delightful spell over me—the smell of printer's ink and newsprint, the slow, bubbling sound of the Linotype's mini caldrons making molten lead into words, the incessant ring of the telephones, the swishing sound of the big flatbed press, my father slipping me a nickel to put in my savings account at the corner bank. "It's for a rainy day," he would say, pretending to admonish me.

And, oh, the museum relics the Times-Call *possessed during the Depression and through the World War II years—naked light bulbs dangling from the high ceiling with strings to pull for making light or darkness in the composing room.*

And next to the windowless east wall stood those three monstrous Linotypes breathing molten lead fumes and clattering as they cast lines of type into slugs of lead for printing. And there the operators sat on low wooden chairs, the legs cut short and reinforced with baling wire, glaring lamp lighting up the keyboard and the copy to be set. A pot of the molten "pigs" (lead bars) fed the whole process, and kept the chill away on wintry days.

To a young boy who slipped back to the pressroom every now and then, the old flatbed press whistled strange tunes as the web of newsprint swished through the many rollers. And there were knocking sounds, too, that echoed down the dark stairs to the basement where the "morgue" was, where they kept the volumes of all the past editions of the paper.

Up front facing Fourth Avenue, a few feet from the downtown fire station, was the newsroom with the sun streaming through the big windows. From the street, as you walked through the front door, and to your left, sat Mary Creese, star reporter, as well as receptionist, and bookkeeper. She also answered the open phone lines.

Across the fenced aisle was the controlling owner and boss, Ray Lanyon, longtime mayor, at his roll-top desk. To me, as a boy, he was old and grumpy at times, but my friend. He saved a rare smile for me when I'd come in to see my father, and he'd nod and wink a secret wink at me. My father said he could gather the facts for a story faster and better than any reporter in the state of Colorado.

Tall, lean Jim Matlack, whose family owned a percentage of the paper, handled the advertising, and laid out the ads on an architect's drawing board with a stool to sit on like Bob Cratchit in Dickens' "A Christmas Carol." He also put out the paper when my father was away on vacation, and covered local stories when needed."

By the early 1900s, Longmont's newspapers were linked to the wider world through wires from the Associated Press, which gave the citizens of Longmont almost instantaneous news from around the country and the world. For instance, an account of the huge earthquake that devastated San Francisco the morning of April 18, 1906, appeared in the *Longmont Daily Times* that very afternoon.

Late-breaking news was often received before publication of the afternoon paper. It was then the custom to post news off the wire in the window of the newspaper offices. To get the Associated Press wire, Ray Lanyon had to convince a number of local businesspeople to invest money to subscribe to the Associated Press stories. Notices of significant news bulletins were literally blasted from a muzzle-loader by Lanyon, who would go out back of the building and shoot his shotgun. The alarm let the townsfolk know they should come to the newspaper office and take a look in the front window where the AP report would be pasted.

Blaine Hayes fitting an aluminum cylinder containing display advertising copy onto a press roller. This was our first step into the "cold type" era, which would eventually completely replace the hot metal and Linotype equipment and processes.

Chapter Twenty-Three

1950s—ON THE BRINK OF PROSPERITY AND GROWTH

LONGMONT HAD ENJOYED MANY YEARS as an agricultural center with productive family farms surrounding the town and providing bucolic buffers against Boulder to the west. To the east, farms stretched into Weld County crossing the Valley Highway, which bisected the state north and south; it was later referred to as Interstate 25 and is now called the "I-25 corridor."

Two important industries spawned by farming were the Great Western Sugar Company and the Empson Canning Factory. Construction of Great Western was completed in 1903 to receive and process the farmers' sugar beets, and it operated well into the 1970s. When it was built, it was said to be the largest of its kind in the world. Empson, which opened in 1887, employed hundreds of residents to can locally grown fruits and vegetables. In the early 1920s, it merged with the Kuner Canning Factory.

Longmont in the 1950s was a fairly quiet place on the brink of growth and prosperity. The newspaper reflected that feeling with a relaxed atmosphere, where press times might be just about any time and circulation numbers were vague. Nobody had any idea who subscribed to the paper.

When Blaine Hayes moved to Longmont in 1952 to take a job as a Linotype operator at the *Times-Call*, he later recalled finding "a town a mile long and a block wide." Main Street, the town's commercial district, was flanked by residential neighborhoods—on the west side along Coffman Street and along the east side on Kimbark Street. Anchored on each end was a Johnson's Corner service station.

Blaine's wife, Alyce, also joined the paper. What began as a part-time job typesetting news and advertising copy quickly turned into thirty-four years working side by side in the production of the newspaper. Later, when Blaine was promoted to composing room foreman, he found himself in charge of supervising his wife at work.

Ray Lanyon hired Hayes by mail. Fresh from service in World War II and recently married, Hayes—like many of his generation—was much more familiar with national and world geography. Returning GIs had discovered there was more to the U.S. than their hometowns, and they were itching to get moving in life. This phenomenon became a statewide trend, according to the Colorado Historical Society, when many veterans relocated to Colorado. Population was growing right along with the federal government, military installations, and scientific institutions throughout the state.

Longmont was home to 8,099 people and boasted at least 25 churches and other services that belied its size. There was a Carnegie library, a museum, and a hospital—all part of a plan, as Betty Ann Newby wrote in her history, *The Longmont Album:* "Much like raising a child without teaching him manners is a city with the technical foundation, and little attention paid to creating a good place to live. Longmont was a planned colony with schools, churches, and parks from its infancy; considerations an unplanned town must add later. An atmosphere for religious, cultural and educational pursuits of its citizens was in place."

The newspaper, although historically indifferent to the rigors of deadlines and press times, was well equipped with a production room containing five Linotype machines. In 1952, for instance, the newspaper was produced on a flatbed press capable of printing an eight-page paper at a rate of 4,500 per hour.

The newspaper's management was interested in commercial printing when Blaine Hayes first joined the staff. Producing business promotional materials and items such as letterheads and envelopes was a priority in the 1950s. The *Times-Call* also printed a monthly publication for Great Western Sugar Company called *Through the Leaves*. The paper itself was very local, full of church and club news, and word from the "chicken dinner circuit" on who was going where and doing what.

The world was deep into the Cold War, and fear of the Russians ran in the nation's consciousness. Sen. Joseph McCarthy began accusing prominent people of being Communists, and the term blacklisting came into being, spawning the term McCarthyism. American officials were warning that foreign bombers could make their way to the United States over the Arctic skies in very short order.

Longmont made national news on March 3, 1952, when the city went through a full-scale mock bombing raid. Bob Coulson, Longmont's civil defense director, oversaw the drill. "I don't think you'd find another town in the whole country that went as far as we did," Coulson said. The *Times-Call* reported, "The siren at the fire station screamed, church bells rang, factory whistles blew and streets were cleared by regular and Civil Defense police."

There were false explosions, and smoke filled the downtown as a B-29 bomber and four P-51 fighter escorts flew 1,000 feet above Main Street. The bomber dropped leaflets with information on what to do in the event of an actual air raid. Dozens of people ran out and dropped on the streets, simulating actual injuries. A 500-bed hospital was set up in the St. Vrain Memorial Building at the corner of Longs Peak Avenue and Coffman Street. "The people in America were war conscious. All over the country they were having air raid drills," Coulson said in recalling that day. "It was the times."

In 1955 a tragedy near Longmont put the city and its newspaper on the map worldwide. On November 2, a United Airlines plane exploded and crashed eight miles northeast of Longmont in western Weld County. The crash, caused by a bomb planted on the plane, killed forty-four on board. International attention became focused on Longmont and its small group of journalists.

The front page of the November 2, 1955, edition of the *Times-Call* brought readers word of the disaster. Reporter Mary Creese rode on a fire engine to the scene where she transmitted details, including eyewitness reports of the crash, to the downtown Longmont newsroom via the fire engine's radio. Jim Matlack, too, arrived quickly on the scene. He reported: "Complete and awful destruction that I hope to never see again littered the fields of the Jake Keil farm when I arrived at the gruesome scene where, less than a half hour before, the United Mainliner had crashed and snuffed out the lives of 44 human beings."

Ultimately, a suspect in the bombing was captured and confessed. John Gilbert Graham claimed he planted the bomb in order to kill his mother and collect $37,500 in life insurance. The *Times-Call* followed the story on through to Graham's trial and execution on January 11, 1957, at the Colorado State Penitentiary in Cañon City. The *Times-Call* received an international award from the Associated Press for its work in helping the world press cover the disaster.

I covered Graham's trial in Denver and discussed various legalities of the case in a regular lawyer's column I wrote for the *Denver Post*. The trial is believed to have been the first with television cameras present.

"Bernie" Faller Sr. received the Associated Press Managing Editors Award for his work in covering the crash, but his efforts didn't stop when the crash coverage faded. In his essay about his father, the younger Faller noted, "Immediately after the tragedy, he began researching the air safety records of Colorado and the nation, made calls to Denver and Washington, D.C., contacted state and national legislators. When he had all his ducks lined up he launched a heated editorial campaign to require inspection of all baggage." While the debate Faller sparked ultimately faded, his efforts and the issue serve as a link between the newspapers of yesterday and today.

However, something happened on October 4, 1957, that changed the greater St. Vrain Valley and the world forever. The Russians launched the world's first satellite, called *Sputnik 1*, the Russian word for *satellite*. It quickly captured the world's attention as it flew high overhead.

The *Times-Call* reported on Earl Morrison, an amateur radio operator who lived four miles southwest of town. Morrison measured the progress of *Sputnik 1* as it moved high above Longmont at 90 to 115 miles per hour. For the next several days, the *Times-Call* was filled with stories about the satellite officially beginning the space race and growing tension with the Soviet Union.

With such apprehension about the Soviets, it was a real jolt to people when they discovered the Russians had beaten the United States into space with *Sputnik 1*. The launch also lit a fire underneath the United States in the space and arms races and led directly to the creation of the National Aeronautics and Space Administration (NASA).

Thinking and attitudes in America underwent a big change after the launch. The country grew increasingly concerned that we were well behind the Russians in mathematics and science education.

Almost overnight, heavy emphasis was placed on capturing the interest and imagination of youth in technology and encouraging the study of the sciences required to place the United States in a competitive position.

Jim Matlack, reporter and one of our company directors, at his desk in the newsroom of the Longmont Times-Call.

I remember some of our young newspaper carriers during this period had to leave their routes because they were getting so much homework assigned at school. We went through a substantial turnover of paper carriers during this period.

Several key employees stayed on after we bought the paper in 1957. Jim Matlack was one of them. It soon became apparent he was a bit of a playboy with an active social life. But we pretended not to notice, and he played right on. We referred to him as our crown prince. One night Ruth and I followed him home from the Elks Club and, while he finally made it home, it was a wild ride getting there. At that time Jim was living at the fire station as he was going through another divorce. However, when the going got tough, he was second to none as a rewrite man and a remarkable newshound.

Mary Creese stayed with us for a short time as our newsroom typist. She was one of the fastest at writing stories. I'm afraid I burned her out on modest corrections. She was known for throwing phone directories around the office regularly at those who questioned her copy. I was surprised I was never hit by one.

Blaine Hayes stayed with the newspaper for thirty-four years as our production manager and was a vice president of Lehman Communications Corporation at the time of his retirement in 1986. His wife, Alyce, retired at the same time. Blaine was a capable and gifted production manager, and his career spanned the hot metal to cold type eras of newspaper production. We had a great association. People often think of the excitement in the newsroom or in the advertising departments without realizing the challenges and stress faced behind the scenes by the production department in producing daily newspapers. Blaine and Alyce Hayes fulfilled dedicated roles for the people of the communities we served.

Ruth and I began to make significant changes and set about putting the business in order. We established deadlines and created separate news, circulation, and accounting departments—all relatively new concepts for the Longmont paper. We also separated the newspaper and commercial operations. However, these ideas were not yet all that important to the paper's employees. Ruth was assertive and direct, and drawn to the intricacies of business organization and accounting procedures. For the first time, employees were given time sheets to record their hours of work.

The newspaper was produced on five Linotypes that set type in metal castings. "Hot metal" referred to the pots of liquid lead that solidified into the lead bars, imprinted with each day's news and advertising text.

Even though I thought I knew where we were going in the newspaper business, we had to really pull our way through many troubles. The equipment was old, and the staff was old. They did things the way they had always done them, and that simply wasn't good enough anymore.

The place had the good atmosphere of old-time newspapers. It smelled of newsprint and the wire service constantly clattered in the background. But we needed desks and equipment, and the lighting was not very good. There was a saw in the back for cutting metal, so the pressmen would move a hanging light over it. Then, just as soon as no one was watching, one of the Linotype operators would come along and move the light back over a layout table. This went on all the time. Finally we installed more modern tube lights.

The newsroom was sort of Dickensian. It was terribly short of space, and the furniture was for the most part small, except for Mr. Lanyon's desk. He had a big roll-top desk where he was always sorting mail. So it was not a very comfortable place. I worked around the roll-top desk for a long time and was never able to get my own desk in the newsroom. Ruth couldn't either, so she worked standing at the front counter.

Things were hard for Ruth at first because Lanyon didn't want her in the plant. He was of the old school. He could not understand women in business and refused to sell any of his stock to a woman. Ironically, Lanyon had mortgaged his home to buy the *Daily Times* from the Beckwiths, and in order to pay the interest and meet the notes he brought his wife into the office where she worked for three years to help him. They dedicated their lives to the paper and to the town.

Lanyon served six terms as mayor and was active in the early promotion of what became the Colorado-Big Thompson Project and other water development. "Where there is water and power, there will be healthy growth," Lanyon said. Longmont and the *Times-Call* proved his premise.

Water was always a topic of concern in the West—due to not enough of it or to the challenges of having to manage too much of it, both of which could be catastrophic depending on the longevity and severity of the conditions. Over the years, the pages of the *Times-Call* frequently described water development and demands. "Big Thompson project water was of great benefit in making good crops possible in the Longmont district," the December 31, 1956, issue reported. A report the year before on December 30, 1955, emphasized the importance of irrigation water:

". . . dryland crops all over the county were very poor due to the lack of carryover moisture from 1953. In the north part of the county, irrigated crops were much better overall than the year before."

An editorial by Ray Lanyon published November 22, 1955, reminded readers of the debt of gratitude they owed those with the foresight to bring water from the Western Slope through the Continental Divide to the Front Range. Lanyon called for the renaming of some of the Colorado-Big Thompson Water Project's features to honor these men.

> *In the past, men of vision have been honored and we might mention that founders of Longmont were remembered when many of our streets were named after them. These include Kimbark, Emery, Baker, Collyer, Coffman, Terry, Pratt, Bross and Gay streets.*
>
> *Those in position to do so should lose no time in bringing about recognition of the leaders who brought into being the Colorado-Big Thompson Diversion Project.*

If Ruth was angered by Lanyon's backward approach to women in business, she got over it. We were undeterred. We would sneak into the plant at night and have a look around. I think it was probably a good thing that much of what Ruth first saw of the *Times-Call* plant was veiled in shadows. Ruth probably would have been more upset if she had seen closer into the nooks and crannies because the physical plant was rather quaint. A sign over the back door to the production department read: "Abandon All Hope Ye Who Enter Here." It was one of those great times when most problems were solved with hot lead (from the Linotype printing process). If there was a hole in the cement floor, someone poured lead in it. If the chairs were falling apart, someone poured hot lead in them and fixed them up.

Ruth asked a family accountant to drive up from Denver to look around. He looked at me in horror and asked, "What have you gotten Ruth into?" He didn't foresee any good outcome for us. He thought it was the greatest lot of wreckage he'd ever seen. Later, Ruth and I were at the Museum of Science and Industry in Chicago where we saw a printing shop from the turn of the century. As we looked at it, our eyes grew wide. I said, "Well, Ruth, that's our plant. That's just the way it looks."

Just as I had, many journalists and entrepreneurs got their start in newspapers at a tender age. The first fall after purchasing the paper, we introduced an independent business system for our youth carriers to circulate the paper. We called it the Little Merchant System. It was a new approach that made carriers independent contractors of the newspaper.

They became an important part of the newspaper and the foundation of the *Times-Call* circulation system. On one occasion they quite literally almost undermined the whole operation. Each day the newspaper carriers came to the alley behind the offices to wait for the papers to roll off the press. They spent a lot of time cooling their heels there because the paper was frequently late in those early days. As a pastime they would pick the concrete out from between the building's bricks. It didn't take long for the entire wall, including the electrical controls for the press, to cave in, causing the paper to be much later than normal that day.

Over time we would have one of the largest youth newspaper carrier teams in the state, including its first female "paperboy." I was glad to have had the background and experience of being a paperboy in my own youth.

I felt a vibrant community and a vibrant community newspaper were closely linked. Back then, everyone in the community came by the *Times-Call* to get their pictures taken with the hopes of getting them published in the paper, which we generally did. From my time on the *Rocky Mountain News* and the *Denver Post*, I remember feeling the newspapers could be doing a lot more than they were doing in the Denver community. I hoped we would play a much greater role in guidance of the Longmont community.

We began by covering the city council meetings and tried to bring a new awareness of politics to the newspaper's pages. In June 1957 the newspaper announced Longmont's hospital fund-raising campaign was a success with construction of a new $850,000 hospital facility to commence the following month.

Ruth played a greater role in the community than I. She was able to help with the start of many good causes, such as the YMCA, the symphony orchestra, art exhibits, and many other civic causes.

Longtime Longmont resident Lea M. Flanders joined the news staff as society editor in December, 1957. She was with us for more than thirty years covering community fund-raising efforts, features about fashion and home décor, and stories of crime and local tragedy.

Flanders and I agreed that people like to read about people, particularly those they know—they are drawn to stories about their friends, neighbors and members of their community. She seemed to have a special formula for getting the community's attention and rallying people behind a cause. She was unrelenting in her writing endeavors, usually ensuring the success of whatever cause was being espoused. This success also translated into numerous professional awards for writing and editing from the Colorado Press Association, Colorado Press Women, and the National Federation of Press Women.

Ruth and I saw the possibility that a newspaper could be a quiet force behind the scenes in community development. On July 1, 1957, we spelled out this belief by announcing a new motto for the newspaper: "To Build a Better World, Start in Your Own Community."

I wrote an editorial explaining the new slogan:

We sincerely feel it contains a thought worthy of consideration by every member and every business in a vigorous, growing city.

Too frequently, every one of us spends hours pondering distant situations and overlooking the local problems that largely are within our control. Naturally, in this world today, it is necessary to consider conditions and circumstances in distant places. Yet it is more important to act, remedy and improve the things going on in our own backyard. . . .

Longmont is blessed with a number of devoted and sincere volunteer workers. These people, who give so freely of their time and thought, cannot do the job alone. They need the help of every person in the community. . . .

Thus, it is with a sense of guidance in the policy of this newspaper, as well as urging healthy, constructive community action that we adopt the theme, "To Build a Better World, Start in Your Own Community."

In 1959 the plant on 655 Fourth Avenue underwent a major internal overhaul. One change was the installation of teletype perforation equipment, which eliminated a time-consuming production step. As the 1950s drew to a close, newspaper operations continued marching toward further modernization.

Chapter Twenty-Four

DENVER REAL ESTATE

MEANWHILE, INTERMINGLED WITH OUR LIVES as newspaper owners were remnants of our life in Denver. And these were by no means minor responsibilities. Although Ruth and I had closed our law practice in Denver, she still owned and managed sizable real estate properties, one of which was her late father's White Truck Company building, located at 18th Avenue and Pearl Street. It was a most unusual property that would become both a massive problem and a tremendous opportunity in the years ahead.

Mountain States Telephone & Telegraph found the building ideal for its operations and decided to lease it. They asked Ruth to supervise remodeling of the premises to their specifications. It was in the basement of this building in the mid-1950s that Ruth and I flirted with death by electrocution as we stood knee-deep in water during a flood. The city had removed the surface of the sidewalks along 18th Avenue in preparation for some street construction, but shortly afterward, there was a tremendous rain. With nowhere to go, the water gushed into the basement, saturating equipment, and disrupting service far and wide, causing telephone bills to be a little late that month.

I made every effort to get the Denver Fire Department to loan us some of their pumper trucks to pump the eighteen inches of water out of the boiler room, but the department could not be without the trucks in case of other emergencies. Fortunately we had understanding tenants, and flooded facilities were not a brand-new experience for them. They quickly put their own huge pumps to work sending the water out of the building. But this was a laborious and slow process as it had to be pumped back into the gutters of 18th Avenue with great care so as not to overload the storm sewers already close to capacity.

Negotiations soon began for the construction of a 31,000-square-foot addition to the north side of the Mountain Bell building. This addition would house new IBM accounting equipment needed to process records of customer-dialed, long-distance calls for the Colorado-Wyoming Accounting Center of Mountain States Telephone & Telegraph. It came to be known as the Pearl Street Building. The design given final approval extended the main building over the adjoining parking lot on elevated pylons, leaving the ground-level parking space intact.

Ruth supervised the construction while I handled negotiations for the 18th Avenue Corporation, which Ruth and I had set up to handle the site's business. It was completed by fall 1959, allowing Mountain States to bring direct dialing to telephone users throughout the Denver metropolitan area.

Years later, in a case of déjà vu, I received a phone call one day from Floyd Sturgeon, then manager of the Longmont Telephone Company, located at the corner of 6th Avenue and Coffman Street. He reported that their building was flooding due to a broken sprinkler head. The Longmont telephone building was only one story high with almost no windows—a contributing factor in the difficulty of getting the water out. Again, the telephone company used its own pumps to remove the water. Service took considerable time to restore as the damaged electrical equipment had to be dried out or replaced. The irony was not lost on me, having been down this soggy road before and knowing all too well the challenge in preventing its recurrence.

Chapter Twenty-Five

1960s—A TIME OF AWAKENING

LONGMONT WAS GROWING. By 1960 the population was 11,489 and the *Times-Call* reflected this growth with a total paid daily circulation that had risen by nearly one-quarter to 4,800. The newspaper had firmly established itself as Longmont's community paper. Local news still reigned, and we were sponsoring a variety of community activities such as golf and ski classes and European travel tours.

The year 1960 was big for the country as well, which had just elected its youngest president, John F. Kennedy. It was also a big year for Colorado. In April our banner headline read "$4 Million Air Traffic Control Center to Be Built at Longmont." Behind the scenes I had been alerted by U.S. Sen. Gordon Allott that the Federal Aviation Administration (FAA) was in search of a suitable location to construct an air traffic control center for its western regional facility. The FAA would bring approximately 200 high-paying jobs to the area, which Longmont badly needed.

I went into action immediately to put together a small group of people to research a suitable site. Longmont Mayor Al Will, Councilman Fred Korte, and Realtor Wade Gaddis met with the FAA to learn more about its needs. With this information in hand, the local Chamber of Commerce was soon on board, leading a campaign to raise money to cover the cost of land and city services.

Late one Thursday afternoon, I received a call from Sen. Allott letting me know that Longmont had been chosen by the FAA, and he inquired about our progress in locating property. As I was giving the good senator the status, he assured me this was no pipe dream. In fact, he said time was extremely short to get this accomplished. As the call ended, I realized I

The newspaper sponsored many community events, including printing Santa letters at Christmas. Children and their parents lined up to give their letters to Santa.

had to work very fast, with only the weekend to pull the deal together. John Meyer at Longmont National Bank, Tom Brock, and Carl Turner of Turner Realty, among others, helped get the work accomplished that weekend.

A farm owned by Colin Stroh appeared to meet all the FAA's requirements. It was just outside city limits on the north side between what is now 16th and 17th Avenues and Hover Road and Francis Street. Four northern Colorado cities had been under consideration, and all had met the necessary criteria, but the final decision came down to the cost of communication lines from Denver. These landlines would link Longmont to areas throughout Colorado and surrounding states in the new network of air traffic control.

The new facility, costing in excess of $1 million, would be a 56,000-square-foot building and contain virtually every known type of communications equipment. It would take about a year to build and another nine months to install all the equipment. Longmont celebrated the dedication of the new FAA facility in 1962.

Meanwhile, flight of another kind was capturing the headlines and imagination of the world. Soviet cosmonaut Yuri Gagarin became the first man to orbit Earth on April 12, 1961, resuming the space race in earnest. NASA had been working on Project Mercury, America's first manned space flight program.

U.S. Astronaut Alan Shepard Jr. was chosen for the first American manned mission into space. After several delays Shepard piloted the *Freedom 7* mission on May 5, 1961, becoming the first American and second person to travel into space on a 15-minute, 22-second suborbital flight. The launch was seen live on television by millions. Just 20 days later, President Kennedy declared the American national space objective was to put a man on the moon. The next space flight was February 20, 1962, when John Glenn became the first American to orbit Earth.

The *Times-Call* discontinued the Saturday afternoon edition in June 1961, replacing it with a morning paper. And, an era truly ended in Longmont when pioneer, politician, and former newspaper publisher Ray Lanyon passed away on October 8, 1961. He had spent fifty-five years with the *Times* and another four as editor emeritus. In a tribute to Lanyon, we wrote, "Ray Lanyon never opposed people—he battled for or against issues . . . (he) opposed the Ku Klux Klan which was in its heyday. He was threatened at the office and at home. A campaign was launched to have subscriptions cancelled. He never relented, however, and weathered the storm. . . . Ray Lanyon was a newspaperman's newspaperman. He was a star reporter, and no greater tribute can be paid to anyone of his profession."

We marked the paper's 75th anniversary on March 17, 1962, by looking forward rather than back. For this occasion, I wrote, "The job before us is to provide an ever improving product to a growing number of residents and subscribers. Whether our roots go back 91 or 75 years does not matter as much as the job we do today and tomorrow."

The recognition of the ever-pressing need to cover the news with care and accuracy was noted with a growing number of awards from press associations. On April 14, 1962, for example, the newspaper received the Arthur A. Parkhurst Trophy for excellence in Colorado daily newspapers. That same year, I received honorable mention in the Ralph L. Crossman editorial writing awards

In 1962, International Business Machines (IBM) was in the early stages of making plans for a new facility. Once again working quietly with

Longmont Times-Call *news editor Tom Reeves preparing a photo for publication.*

a small group of city officials, local Realtors, bankers, and IBM managers, I helped locate 660 acres of farmland strategically situated between Boulder and Longmont that IBM could use. Longmont leaders slowly began to see the merit in working to attract more large-scale technology firms similar to IBM.

During the building phase, IBM was extremely secretive about what was going on at the site, which stimulated much speculation. Many people

Longmont Times-Call *paperboys preparing their papers for daily delivery in the 1960s, directed by Bob Cook, center in tie and sweater, and Jerry Reeves in press apron.*

thought it might be an automobile factory. In 1965 IBM opened its new manufacturing plant. The plant would forever change the city and the surrounding area, sparking population and business growth that reverberated for decades.

IBM's presence and the population growth that followed brought water issues again to the forefront. The newspaper reported the Water Advisory Board's unflinching announcement that the city's water supplies would be exhausted within a few short years if new water development did not immediately take place.

As town and newspaper grew side by side, the newspaper's circulation grew to 6,000 by 1963.

A newcomer joined the "staff". Although not an actual person, *Johnnie St. Vrain* emerged as an advocate for Longmont in the form of a daily column that answered questions from readers on hundreds of topics ranging from pothole problems to local government issues. The popular column has continued for decades to this day, written by many different

Bob Cook, Longmont Times-Call *circulation manager, making last-minute route changes at his desk.*

people including managing editors, city editors, editorial board members, reporters, administrative assistants, and myself.

In September 1964, with increasing circulation and news pages, the company completed a new 11,000-square-foot building on the southeast corner of Fourth Avenue and Terry Street.

By 1966 the paper was reporting that the North Vietnamese had attacked a U.S. destroyer in the Gulf of Tonkin, spurring the change in the military's role in Vietnam from adviser to participant.

In 1967 I was honored as Colorado's Outstanding Publisher of the Year by the Colorado Press Association. In my Editor's Notepad column of April 2, 1967, I wrote:

I welcomed the public at the front door of the newly built facility on 717 Fourth Avenue.

Indians and grasshoppers reportedly were the settlers' big problems in 1860 when only two or three log houses appeared in the St. Vrain Valley.

Eleven years later, on April 26, 1871, our founding publisher Elmer F. Beckwith stressed the changes in the newspaper's first edition. He wrote in 1871:

The move to 717 Fourth Avenue included a new press. The newspaper could now be printed on a hot metal rotary press with faster speed than the old flatbed press at 655 Fourth Avenue.

"Go where you will, you find mile after mile of fencing, ditches built all over the face of the country, and bringing land under ditch where it was supposed water would never run."

On July 1, 1871, the new town of Longmont, Colorado Territory was the subject of an extensive pamphlet published by the Chicago-Colorado Colony which reported:

"From the first of March, 1871, down to the present time, the growth of the colony has been steadily progressive. Scarcely a day has passed, but one or more colonists have arrived on the ground, selected their lots and lands, and set about improving them to their own liking."

Tom Reeves and I were present to receive a Community Service Award at the Colorado Press Association Convention held in Denver in February 1967. Two years later, the Longmont Daily Times-Call received recognition from peers and industry associations with the prestigious Community Service Award bestowed by the University of Missouri's School of Journalism in an annual competition sponsored by the Chicago-based Inland Press Association.

Civilization was moving at a faster pace when colonization began almost a century ago. Before that point in time, the area had been a vast territory inhabited by Indians, trappers, explorers and then a wave of gold seekers. Following the tide of those searching for gold came the more permanent settlers. In 1858, one of the first pioneer settlers was John Ramsay Rothrock. He and his group of 13, traveled westward along the St. Vrain River. Their welcoming committee proved to be Chief Left Hand and a band of Arapahoe Indians. The Indians were hostile and armed.

Chief Left Hand whose Indian name was "Niwot" gestured that the white men should leave.

"White man come to kill our game, to burn our wood, to destroy our grass," Chief Left Hand accused.

There soon followed a pow-wow finished by the smoking of a pipe of peace. A solemn agreement was reached: "The Indian and the white man shall forever live together in peace." And essentially, the spirit of this covenant remained.

Drought and grasshoppers proved far greater challenges to the settlers than scattered incidents with Indians. The community actually began at Burlington, on the banks of the St. Vrain River. This first 'rooting' of the community changed after January, 1871 when three men—H. D. Emery, Sidney Gay and Seth Terry—arrived from Chicago to choose new land where a city should be built. They chose the present town site to the north of Burlington. Little by little, the town of Burlington was abandoned as its residents moved to Longmont.

In 1946, the entire area joined in a series of massive programs to salute Longmont's 75th anniversary. In 1967, preliminary planning already is underway for the 100th birthday celebration to be held in just four years.

The St. Vrain Valley has a rich history and its people have a deep appreciation for the early day settlers who braved many perils and hardships to build the foundations upon which it flourishes today.

Chapter Twenty-Six

EXPANSION TO THE NORTH—
LOVELAND

IN MAY 1967, Ruth and I completed the purchase of another daily newspaper located in the town of Loveland, just 18 miles north of Longmont. With a population of approximately 5,000 and a newspaper circulation of less than 4,000, Loveland was also a rural farming area but fast turning into a retirement destination for many farmers from Kansas, Nebraska, and other Midwestern states.

The *Loveland Reporter-Herald* was combined with the *Longmont Times-Call* as separate divisions—the Loveland Publishing Company and Times-Call Publishing Company, respectively. Jack Holden, editor and publisher, agreed to stay on. It was our sincere belief that we could better serve our respective communities by combining our management forces. By doubling the skills and enriching the creative ranks of management personnel, both newspapers and both communities would benefit. Combining the two historic newspaper publishing properties had been under consideration for many years. The *Reporter-Herald* was in its 88th year and the *Times-Call* in its 96th year of community publication.

Our policy was, "Under the new arrangement, both newspapers will operate with complete independence in editorial policy. It will be determined solely at the local level, by local people.

"Both newspapers will do their very best to forward the interests of their respective communities. However, on matters of mutual or area wide interest, both publications will combine to forward the causes of this great area of Colorado." At the time, printing and publication operations were kept in the individual communities.

The Daily Reporter-Herald, *pictured here in 1983, was located in this 10,000-square-foot plant at 450 N. Cleveland Avenue, in downtown Loveland. Begun in 1880, the newspaper served the people of Loveland and the area extending from Estes Park in the Rocky Mountains to the adjoining plains communities along the Front Range.*

Holden's father, Harley E. Holden, a former Kansas publisher, had purchased the *Reporter-Herald* in 1944 from R. J. Ball, editor, and R. L. Etter, advertising manager. Ball had been a major influence in Colorado journalism and served as president of the Colorado Press Association in 1931 and 1932. In 1948 Jack Holden joined his father at the paper.

Loveland's first newspaper, *The Reporter*, was founded in 1880 by G. N. Udell—almost nine years after the paper in Longmont—with the motto "Independent in all things, neutral in nothing." Within a couple of years, it was sold to Frank A. McClellan, the eldest son and founder of the *Larimer County Express*, which had been established in April 1873.

In the forty years between 1882 and 1922, *The Reporter* changed ownership seven times and relocated four times. *The Loveland Leader*, a weekly that started up in 1883, was sold to *The Reporter* that same year.

The Loveland Register entered the local newspaper market in 1884, delivering competition to *The Reporter. The Register* changed hands several times before being renamed the *Daily Herald* in 1908.

In celebration of the Loveland Daily Reporter-Herald's *125th anniversary in 2005 we produced a commemorative book titled* Loveland Publishers and Pioneers *providing a snapshot of the past, present, and future of the Loveland community. This composite photo of the newly merged* Reporter *with the* Daily Herald *spawned the* Reporter-Herald *and* Weekly Reporter *as it appeared in 1922, at left. The* Loveland Daily Reporter-Herald *building, at right, was constructed in 1994. The newspaper continued the proud tradition of reporting the news. Through floods and fires, triumphs and tragedies we brought the world to the doors of Loveland and surrounding communities.*

By 1920 *The Reporter* moved from a tri-weekly publication to a daily production cycle, and the *Daily Herald* was purchased and merged with it. In time, the paper became the *Daily Reporter-Herald*.

In 1956 the paper's facilities were moved to 450 North Cleveland Avenue, at the southeast corner of Fifth Avenue and Cleveland. Within three years Harley E. Holden sold his interest in the newspaper to Harlow E. Tibbetts, also a former Kansas publisher. Tibbetts co-published with Jack Holden until Tibbetts' sudden death in January 1962. Holden then became both publisher and editor in chief. He sold his remaining interest in the paper to us in June 1969, and I became publisher of the *Loveland Daily Reporter-Herald* in addition to the *Longmont Daily Times-Call*. Tom Reeves moved from Longmont to Loveland to become its general manager and editor.

In 1967 the Longmont and Loveland daily newspapers merged. Shown seated are John E. Holden, editor and publisher of the Loveland Daily Reporter-Herald, *and Edward Lehman, editor and publisher of the* Longmont Daily Times-Call. *Standing from left are H. R. Holliday, advertising director and vice president of the* Reporter-Herald; *Ruth G. Lehman, secretary-treasurer of the Times-Call Publishing Company and the Loveland Publishing Company; and James F. Matlack,* Times-Call *associate editor and vice president, and a director of both publishing companies.*

In the summer of 1968, I made preparations for attending the National Republican Convention in Miami, Florida.

Overseas the Vietnam War was not going well for the U.S. During the Vietnamese holiday of Tet on January 30-31, 1968, Viet Cong units blanketed South Vietnam with a series of shock attacks in 7 of the largest cities and numerous provincial capitals from the Delta to the demilitarized zone. By the end of the fighting, more than 32,000 Viet Cong troops had been killed and almost 6,000 captured. More than 350,000 civilians became new refugees in addition to the 800,000 refugees officially reported prior to January 30. Although the attack was considered a failure for the Viet Cong, almost 4,000 U.S. soldiers and nearly 5,000 South Vietnamese troops were killed, further weakening support at home for the war.

In August 1968, Gordon Gauss, Colorado Associated Press statehouse and political reporter, and I traveled to Miami to cover the Colorado delegation at the National Republican Convention. At the time, I called it "the year of the unexpected." I felt the Republican candidates reflected their constituents in Colorado, and I looked forward to bringing the story to our readers in explaining their differences and how they would represent Colorado if elected.

I also attended the Democratic National Convention in Chicago, and I couldn't have been more right about it being a year of the unexpected. However, I never in my wildest dreams would have imagined what took place in Chicago that year. While most of the "action" was taking place outside the convention hall, heated arguments and even some fistfights were erupting inside. Still, in the founding of this nation, similar events took place as our Declaration of Independence and U.S. Constitution were drafted.

Chapter Twenty-Seven

1970s—GROWING INTO A NEW GENERATION

AS WE EMBARKED ON A NEW DECADE Mother's health deteriorated rapidly and she passed away at the age of 84. She had lived a rather remarkable life, much of it on her own terms. Mother had made a successful real estate career at a time when most women had not yet stepped into establishing business professions of their own.

In just ten years, Longmont's population had doubled from what it had been in 1960, to 23,209. The Kuner-Empson cannery closed its doors, bringing to an end 83 years of canning the produce of area farms and employing many residents of the Greater St. Vrain Valley.

Professionally I was honored to be elected president of the Colorado Press Association (CPA) in 1970, following in Ray Lanyon's large footsteps; he had been CPA president in 1931. In speaking to a group of past CPA presidents, Lanyon had stated, "Lehman wants me to stick around in an advisory capacity. . .he hasn't mentioned anything about a salary." He was interrupted by a voice from the rear saying, "Don't give him much advice then, Ray."

A brand-new technology called "cold type" was being introduced to the newspaper industry. Our papers began the process of moving out of the hot metal era and into the computer age. Photographic processes and computers replaced the remaining Linotypes.

With a $100,000 investment, we began the first stage of this renovation process. A 20,000-square-foot addition was built at the *Times-Call* in 1972-1973 to accommodate a four-unit Goss Urbanite press, capable of printing 32 pages in black, and to modernize the production area. With the new press installation, we shut down the press at the *Reporter-Herald* in order to centralize all of our printing operations on the more modern Goss.

In 1973 the Longmont Daily Times-Call *proceeded with more plant remodeling, adding 20,000 square feet, which included a press hall to accommodate a newer, partial double-deck Goss Urbanite press. Up-to-date computer systems also were installed bringing streamlined printing technology to the Greater St. Vrain Valley.*

Much of the credit for turning the growth of the 1960s into a picture of prosperity in the 1970s belonged to Bob Cook, whom we hired in 1962 as our circulation manager. He was with us for 34 years and was a vice president of Lehman Communications Corporation at the time of his retirement in 1996.

In 1970 circulation stood at approximately 97 percent of the 7,557 occupied households in Longmont. The remainder of the 10,500 total circulation figure was distributed throughout the St. Vrain Valley. Circulation at the *Times-Call* grew steadily in the 1970s. In September 1972, circulation was 12,000. A year later, in November the number reached 13,000. On March 27, 1976, circulation exceeded 14,000 and we all celebrated. By March 15, 1977, the number was 14,627. By August 26, 1977, the *Times-Call* passed a long-time circulation goal of 15,000, hitting 15,009. Later in the year I wrote with elation and gratitude that the newspaper's circulation had hit 16,023. Longmont's population was now 38,500.

Capable of printing 20,000 copies per hour, the Goss Urbanite press increased the newspaper's page capacity to 32 pages.

Each paper conducted department head meetings daily at 9:05 a.m. to discuss that day's production topics, circulation status, press schedules, breaking and top news items, and plans for upcoming commercial projects. In this photo are our department heads and managers, at right side of table from top are Bob Black, production supervisor; Ruth Lehman, associate editor; Ed Lehman, editor and publisher; Tom Reeves, Reporter-Herald *general manager and editor; Blaine Hayes, production manager/vice president; and Bruce Hotchkiss,* Times-Call *managing editor. At top left standing is Dale Carr, pressroom manager; Bill Johnson, director of sales/vice president; Bernie Woltje, advertising manager; Paul Merritt, controller; and lower left, Bob Cook, circulation manager.*

Two of the top news stories of the early 1970s were Project 75 and Vance Brand's space flight. Longmont embarked on Project 75, which was a new city government complex consisting of a new library, Civic Center, and police station. It was completed in 1975, the same year that Longmont-native Vance Brand flew on the *Apollo-Soyuz* mission linking American and Soviet spacecraft.

Nationally in the 1970s, the voting age was lowered to 18 with the passage of the 26th Amendment to the U.S. Constitution; the Beatles went their separate ways; Walt Disney World opened on October 1, 1971, in Orlando, Florida; and mass murderer Charles Manson was sentenced to death. In February 1972, President Richard Nixon became the first U.S.

I generally attended the annual American Newspaper Publishers Association Conference (ANPA). In 1975 President Gerald Ford spoke to us. I am at the top far left.

president to visit Communist China. His conferences with Mao Tse-tung and other Chinese leaders were considered a breakthrough in relations between the two countries. Nixon's trip also opened China to tourism. In November Nixon was reelected to a second term in a landslide victory over Democratic candidate George McGovern.

By 1973 political storm clouds were gathering as the Watergate scandal continued to grow. In Florida President Nixon told newspaper managing editors at an Associated Press meeting, "I am not a crook," but by August 9, 1974, he was forced to resign rather than face impeachment over continuing Watergate revelations.

By the spring of 1975, we were finding the volume of business heavy but manageable. All in all, life was wonderful at this point. I had a magnificent wife; two wonderful children, Dean and Ruthann, who both worked at the paper during summer breaks and who would help direct it in the future, and a fascinating business. There was never a dull moment, and we always seemed to be rushing just to stay above the torrent. While business continued to be good, it was far from the growth patterns we had experienced in the past.

As chairman of the Inland Daily Press Association—a group of mostly family-owned newspapers throughout the Midwest and several other states—I often traveled to Chicago for board meetings. With only four months to go in this office, I fully grasped all the sweeping changes that had been made during my years in the organization, including firmly establishing the Inland Foundation.

In those years, I devoted much time to organizations, such as the Inland Foundation, and met and served with many wonderful people. In addition, I was a trustee of the University of Denver. It was all a great education, but it was also a great sacrifice on Ruth's part. Lots of new machinery was delivered into Longmont and Loveland at this time, and the *Reporter-Herald* plant in Loveland was undergoing major remodeling. We had been treading water far too long on major internal decisions and expansion plans. So I felt it was time to draw some of these volunteer jobs to a close and took a major step forward when I decided not to become president of the Inland Foundation. Ruth and I decided our future would begin when these activities were concluded, giving us more time to focus on our own business pursuits.

As 1975 passed into history, I recalled what a significant year it had been: The Vietnam War officially ended on April 30 as North Vietnamese troops seized the capital of South Vietnam, completing the Communist takeover. The scene of the last Americans and some of their Vietnamese allies departing Saigon by helicopter from the U.S. Embassy's rooftop remains a fixed image of the end of the war in many Americans' minds. In addition, a federal jury in Sacramento, California, found Lynette "Squeaky" Fromme, a follower of Charles Manson, guilty of trying to assassinate President Gerald Ford in September 1975. Moviegoers were scared by Jaws; Atari developed the first home video games; and mood rings and videocassette recorders (VCRs) came into vogue.

Shortly into 1976 Ruth and I hired a new secretary, Debby Fitzgerald, realizing our office systems were in a state of complete collapse. In just two weeks we made more progress than during the previous four months. At the newspapers, business was good. Paid circulation in 1976 in Loveland was over 11,000 and Longmont topped 14,000.

With his new diploma from Denver University, Dean began covering the 1976 session of the Colorado State Legislature. It was a new adventure for him that I was sure would prove to be a worthwhile experience in the years to come.

Developments at the American Newspaper Publishers Association (ANPA) forced me to disclose that I was not planning to continue on the board after my term ended in April 1977. It came as a shock to the board, and I too had some regrets. However, in the long run, I knew it was the right decision. I knew there would be many new major responsibilities creating deep demands on my time and pockets.

I also made a great personal discovery at the ANPA convention in Las Vegas that summer. I came to the realization that I was dull and completely uncreative when it came to having a good time or experiencing the more exciting things of life. In my very young years, it was I who knew the exciting and most unusual things to do. Now others were doing the exciting things, such as Outward Bound, floating rivers, and traveling in Europe. Fortunately, while we were in Las Vegas, John M. Jones of Greenville, North Carolina, took me to a show featuring comedians Carol Burnett and Tim Conway. Once there, I enjoyed it immensely, but it was a real lesson. I never would have gotten there on my own. Perhaps this was like flying, which I didn't do until I was pushed into it in 1965. Since then I have enjoyed flying hundreds of thousands of miles.

The Las Vegas convention was where I learned many new things, chief among them to reaffirm my dedication to being not merely a good editor, but an exceptional one. The most important of all discoveries was "to know thyself"—learning my own weaknesses as well as my strengths.

I also took a two-day course in Denver at the University of Colorado's Business School on time management, which had been of growing concern to me. I was determined to put this new philosophy into action and increase my effectiveness.

As Ruth and I marked our twenty-seventh wedding anniversary on April 22, 1976, we noted how different and unexpected the path our lives had taken—more so than we ever could have foreseen back in 1949.

We lived in a surging sea with many tugs and pulls. As the tide ebbed and flowed at the Longmont plant, we experienced many new production highs with updated equipment now capable of setting type at 60 lines per minute compared to a journeyman Linotype operator's production of 3 to 3.5 lines of type per minute. And, in 1976 the *Times-Call* became the first news outlet in the area, and the only one between Kansas City and California, capable of electronic transmission of photographs via Laserphoto equipment.

The newspaper business was very good, but there were constant challenges. At the same time, we were on the brink of many personnel changes in Longmont at the *Times-Call*. We experienced turnovers in several positions: the librarian, the education/police reporter, the news department secretary, and an administrative assistant. And, we were experiencing a startling series of absences and vacations.

We operated a vigorous internship program with the journalism departments at the University of Colorado in Boulder and Colorado State University in Fort Collins, which helped to augment the newsroom staffs. However, relying on interns could leave us particularly vulnerable at semester breaks or beginning and end of school terms when students graduated or simply moved on to full-time employment elsewhere. Depending on the time of year and coupled with normal turnover, these upheavals could considerably deplete our newsroom staffs.

The Bicentennial celebration of the Declaration of Independence and America's founding as a free nation was a very exciting occasion, as people throughout the country observed July 4, 1976. Television showed festivities in major cities across the country, led by the armada of sailing ships in New York Harbor. I was pleased we produced Bicentennial editions in Longmont and Loveland dedicated to this historic event.

The Bicentennial provided a real opportunity for many to rededicate themselves to the cause of our free nation. With all our problems, the basic structure still assured freedom. We do have debate and free discussion of our problems. In other countries, such debate is downright dangerous, if not impossible. Our freedom continually gives birth to fresh leadership. One of the great characteristics of our fellow citizens is the firm belief that each person can do the job better than the boss or leader. Amazingly, this is often quite true.

Many of the problems we faced in 1976 will be improved or become obsolete by 2076, but there always will be new problems. In a democracy such as ours, there continually will be deep issues confronting this country's citizens. After all, despite disappointments in leadership and representation, the power really does rest with the people, and ultimately they must make the decisions to remedy them.

Having lived a quarter of the time of this great nation, I was most grateful to have had many opportunities and happy I could pass these benefits along to my children and grandchildren.

Chapter Twenty-Eight

WHEN THE RIVERS ROARED!

BY 10:15 P.M. ON SATURDAY, JULY 31, 1976, reports from Tom Reeves left little doubt that a major disaster was taking place west of Loveland. In just one hour, fourteen inches of rain had fallen in an area near the small mountain hamlet of Glen Haven, sending a 19-foot wall of water crashing down Big Thompson Canyon.

That night Ruthann and I drove up to Loveland in the rain via Interstate 25 and U.S. Highway 34, where we met with a startled *Reporter-Herald* newsroom staff and began to put our emergency plans into operation. Lee Spaulding, managing editor, set up a cot in the newsroom and stayed all night monitoring the police scanner. Finally, he just began taping it so we wouldn't miss anything.

Suddenly we were faced with a number of logistical problems we had never encountered before. They involved the largest news operation we had ever mounted in what came to be described as a 100-year flood.

We soon recognized the need for wide area coverage. Big Thompson Canyon was completely impassable. The river rushed out of the canyon mouth and covered the rural countryside along the Front Range, including parts of the city of Loveland as it spread eastward into the outlying farmland, leaving death and destruction along its path.

To cope, we decided to pool the news and photography resources we had between the two daily papers, with staggered shifts to give relief and yet allow for round-the-clock coverage. By 3 a.m. Ruthann and I were back home and leaving again at dawn to continue action.

Time was our friend and our foe. The weekday editions—we still published six days a week, not yet having begun Sunday morning papers—

were on afternoon press schedules, with the exception of Saturday mornings, giving us about thirty-six hours to set up and begin implementing emergency changes to normal operations.

Making a consistent plan was most worthwhile, and went up and down the line from news and advertising to production and distribution. Deadlines were moved up on all advertising and non-flood-related news content, allowing us to get these pages produced a full day ahead and giving news staff the extra time to compile the latest breaking flood coverage. By Sunday afternoon, August 1, which happened to be Colorado's Centennial, most production was completed for the Monday editions of the *Times-Call* and *Reporter-Herald*.

In terms of newspaper production, we always felt we were keeping up with technology changes in our industry, but the Big Thompson flood happened prior to communication innovations that are largely taken for granted today. The Internet was not yet a twinkle in anyone's eye, and items such as cell phones and laptops—all capable of transmitting breaking news stories and photos from the field—were not yet a part of our arsenal of tools.

Doppler radar was not yet available to the National Weather Service, either. However, this storm, at the outer limits of the 120-mile radar range in Limon, contained an enormous amount of precipitation at both mid and upper levels. Although forecasters couldn't tell how much rain was falling, the sheer size of the storm and the amount of moisture in the air should have shown up on their regular radar screens, but for some reason did not.

Many things went very well, and many could have gone better, at the papers. Our command echelon learned much, and we certainly would be better equipped in the future. In a massive operation of this kind, the planning and logistics at the top are most important. There always are many willing hands, but very close direction is required.

One major shortcoming was transportation. We lacked appropriate vehicles for reporters and photographers for travel on rough terrain. State Highways 7 and 36 through the town of Lyons, west of Longmont, were the only available routes to Estes Park. But once in Estes Park, reporters and photographers had to make their way on foot to Glen Haven, due to impassable roadways.

Dean stayed several weeks in what had once been the carriage house at the Stanley Hotel, located just over a ridge of mountains from Glen

Haven. He filed stories each day by Telecopier, giving us 24-hour coverage and eliminating a daily drive to Estes Park. Dean and Ruthann also coordinated opening an Estes Park News Bureau for the *Reporter-Herald* to better serve the people of Estes Park and its surrounding communities.

Our motor route carriers found delivering papers a monumental task for many months due to the damage to roads and bridges. Although we continued to operate on early deadlines for a couple of weeks, delivery was often late as we continued deep in the midst of news-gathering operations in the flood's aftermath.

One day a circulation truck was in a wreck in Berthoud. That same afternoon a bomb threat was phoned in to the *Times-Call*. Just a few additional problems to add to the day!

Our efforts had been unending, and I feared we had just seen the opening week of a long, long trial. Amazingly, we sold $1,500 in single-copy newspaper sales in Loveland that first week, and over 24,000 copies of original and reprints of the August 2 (Monday) edition. The public had a great need for information about the flood and all that followed.

In late August I drove to the Loveland home of Tom Reeves, and we took a circulation truck into the Big Thompson Valley. The Valley revisited—our staffs wrote millions of words and we published countless photos. Our lives would never be quite the same.

The canyon was so isolated that no one outside those steep walls knew what horrendous events took place that night except for those who had lived through it, Reporter-Herald staff writer Kate Martin wrote of that fateful night:

> *Mike Fink remembers the Big Thompson flood every time he drives up the canyon. His eyes take a distant cast as he remembers the night he and 25 others spent 16 hours huddled under a rock ledge above the raging river.*
>
> *He picks out the spot immediately, near U.S. 34's mile marker 73.*
>
> *"It seemed like a pretty easy climb," Fink says. "I'm amazed, now that I look at it, that we were ever able to make it up. ... The rain was harder than I'd ever seen it rain before or since," Fink said. "The windshield wipers couldn't keep up."*
>
> *About a mile past Waltonia, the storm unleashed a deluge. Large boulders rolled onto the highway and blocked traffic.*

Fink could go no further. He turned his Vega and followed about 10 other cars down the canyon. A half mile later, they ran into a gully washer at True Gulch that they dared not cross. ... "When the water was 1 foot below the road, we decided to get out," Fink said. "We wanted to be prepared just in case." ... Finally, someone in the group suggested they climb the hillside. All of them took shelter between two vertical slabs of rock, about 20 feet above the road. Fifteen minutes later, the river swept their cars away.

"We were trying not to get scared," Fink said. "We guessed there had to be people in the cars and the motor homes."

The roar of the river was so loud they had to shout to be heard. Lightning struck continuously. It was almost like daylight in the canyon, Fink said. . . .

Dave Viegut, then 19, sat on the ridge by the Devil's Backbone to watch the Big Thompson River near midnight Saturday, July 31.

His father, Darrell Viegut, a reserve officer with the Loveland Police Department, handed him a spotlight to search the water's surface for cars, floating debris and bodies. The entire valley was inundated with water. Glade Road and U.S. 34 were underwater, a nearby mobile home park, gone.

After midnight, officials found the first victim.

Viegut left the hillside and went to work for Hunter Funeral Home, where he apprenticed.

At dawn, Fink understood why he felt vibrations in the earth throughout the night. Boulders as big as bulldozers rested in the river's bed where the road used to be. The road was gone in both directions as far as they could see.

Fink said almost everyone was shivering and in the first stages of hypothermia. They broke into a small cabin, which no longer stands, to get blankets and search for food. Later that morning, the group flagged down a rescue helicopter with sheets from the cabin.

Women, children and the elderly were evacuated first. Fink and the other men in the party were airlifted to a small stretch of U.S. 34 that remained and later to Drake. Fink rode with a few others on a four-wheel-drive trail near Storm Mountain. He was dropped off at Loveland High School, a staging area for victims and their families, to reunite with his terrified wife and niece.

"They kept saying they heard different stories of what happened to us," Fink said. "They heard there was another flood coming."

Loveland's heart rose with the need. Thousands of people wanted to help. The National Guard, police officers, firefighters, helicopter pilots, search and rescue personnel and their dogs, reporters and sightseers descended upon Loveland.

Funeral home workers from surrounding communities came to Loveland to help grieving families put their loved ones to rest. Many morticians worked from 8 a.m. to 4 a.m. the following day, Viegut said. They slept at the funeral home and worked in the same clothes day after day.

"I thought I was a big, strong, tough kid," Viegut said, emotion filling his voice. "About three weeks into it, we had a body come in and it was a little 3-year-old boy, and I just lost it."

"Our little town of Sweetheart City woke up," Viegut said. "We are not immune to anything."

Reporter-Herald reporter Sara Hammer wrote of the dangers and obstacles faced nonstop for two weeks by one rescue and recovery operator:

Thirty-one-year-old Fort Collins helicopter pilot Larry Hansen spent two weeks flying in and out of the Big Thompson Canyon in the summer of '76. First he collected survivors; then he returned for the dead.

"It kind of took me back to my military days responding to a military disaster," he said. Hansen, a contract pilot for the Larimer County Sheriff's Department, responded the morning after the July 31, 1976, flood to begin rescue efforts. Each day from dawn to dusk he repeated the trip hundreds of times.

"We assumed there were a lot of people who were hurt. But they either were dead or were fine," he said. "I don't recall ever flying out a person who was hurt.

"We picked people off the top of buildings. We picked people off the sides of cliffs."

Survivors, wondering when their turn to escape would arrive, waved to Hansen as he flew overhead.

"What we were trying to do was get to the ones who looked like they were in worst need, like the ones clinging to rocks or little kids, women. We had the priorities set up," he said.

The memory of one man seeking help stuck out in Hansen's mind.

"This guy, I'd passed over him several times. I'm sure others did, too." Hansen finally landed on the bridge where the man was stranded. The older man boarded the helicopter and explained to Hansen why he was in the canyon.

A volunteer firefighter who lived near the mouth of the canyon, the man received a call about the flood. He was driving to the flood when the water hit the truck. He jumped and ran up the side of the mountain. He spent the night under a small tree and returned to the bridge the next morning.

"He went back down when he got out and went to look for his family. As it turned out, he lost his whole family. He lost his wife, his kids and grandkids who were visiting," Hansen said.

"In the beginning when we saw bodies, we just left them," Hansen said. He spotted victims wrapped in trees and debris, tangled in cars and wedged between rocks. The search for dead took them all the way east to Interstate 25.

Hansen said he received some criticism from onlookers who disliked the method of flying the dead out of the canyon: They had to use a cargo hook and *"sling them out."* Officials moved the landing site near Sylvan Dale and blocked the highway from onlookers.

Hansen recalled the openness of the canyon when he flew in for the first trip. Trees, grass and shrubs as well as houses and other buildings were washed away.

"Where all these things had been there was nothing, absolutely nothing," he said.

A typical month of flying for Hansen is about 100 hours. Two weeks in 1976, he spent 86 hours in the Big Thompson Canyon.

Our hearts were deeply saddened by the loss of life. We were warned that many of those missing might never be found. Tom Reeves looked tired and had many sad thoughts. I feared both Loveland and Estes Park had some bad days ahead. Undoubtedly there would be an economic downturn, and with bodies in seven freezer trailers, soon to be expanded into four refrigerated railroad cars, a pall rested upon the area.

Reporter-Herald reporter Mark Humbert wrote of Daniel Jones and his construction crew who played an enormous role in getting the canyon reopened between Loveland and Estes Park in record time.

> *The Big Thompson Flood brought Daniel Jones to the Loveland area Aug. 2, 1976.*
>
> *He moved here for good the next year.*
>
> *He was one of the first people in the canyon after the flood, "and probably the only one who made it clear through," he said.*
>
> *Jones worked for Green Construction Co. and was in Frisco July 31, 1976. On Aug. 2, he was in his bulldozer pointed up the canyon. The morning after the flood his supervisor had told his crew of eight or nine construction workers "to pack suitcases: We were going in," said Jones.*
>
> *"A lot of people in Estes Park, Drake and Cedar Cove were told that it would be six months before the road would be repaired," he said. "We had traffic up to Cedar Cove in three weeks. They couldn't believe we could rebuild the road that fast."*
>
> *He said that as he worked his way up the canyon, the people shouted and yelled encouragement.*
>
> *"I felt like Patton—like a conquering hero."*
>
> *Jones said his crew worked seven days a week, 12 hours a day, for seven weeks.*
>
> *"Our world for that seven weeks was the canyon," and the site on Carter Lake where they spent their nights*

On Saturday, August 28, Tom and I had a sunny, early fall morning in which to walk. We felt the awe-inspiring message of nature in the sheer rock narrows. Gigantic earthmoving equipment was all about the streambed and pioneer dirt roadway. We could only get so far on foot, so we hitched a ride in a Dodge power wagon owned by Uncle Sam and driven by Gordon Brothers, a claims agent for the Small Business

The alluvial fan is shown as it spread into Horseshoe Park shortly after the Lawn Lake dam breach July 15, 1982. (Kenneth Jessen, photographer. Special to the Loveland Daily Reporter-Herald)

Administration. He drove over the river in unbelievable places to get to sites of loss. Many images flashed back vividly in my mind:

- The incredible destruction and almost 3½ feet of debris in what few standing buildings were left in the small town of Cedar Cove;
- Grandpa's Retreat, located in a deep bend in the river where the sheer rock wall behind the site left people no path of escape;
- The image of the photographer with the six-shooter riding easily on his left hip.

When all the data was collected for the 1976 Big Thompson flood, the death toll came to 144, with 88 injured. Seven people were never found. There were 316 houses and 45 mobile homes destroyed, with 52 businesses and 438 automobiles washed away. Total damage was estimated at more than $35.5 million. The *Reporter-Herald* received recognition for journalistic service from the Associated Press in New York City for its effort in telling this horrific story.

Elkhorn Avenue, Estes Park's main street, was submerged with fast running water filled with debris and mud from the Lawn Lake dam collapse in July 1982. (Loveland Daily Reporter-Herald photo*)*

In the midst of tragedy, and as people and communities struggled to get back to some kind of "normal," life continued on. Dean's departure for law school left the Estes Park news bureau completely unhinged. We had to apply some creative thought and effort in reestablishing the base there. *Reporter-Herald* management needed to be encouraged to take a greater leadership role in coordinating and sustaining the news, advertising, and circulation efforts already begun in this bureau.

Remarkably, six years later, on July 15, 1982, a manmade dam collapsed on Lawn Lake, a high mountain reservoir located at the headwaters of the Big Thompson River just below Mummy Peak in Rocky Mountain National Park. Water contained in this 48-acre lake burst down the banks of the Roaring River, bringing with it a landslide of boulders, rocks, sand, and trees, which formed an alluvial fan as it spread out into Horseshoe Park. A man camped just below the dam was killed.

As the waters moved east out of Horseshoe Park, they began to accumulate behind a 17-foot-high dam on Cascade Lake. The pressure proved too much for this structure and it soon gave way, sending a wall of water through the Aspenglen Campground, killing two campers there.

The town of Estes Park was next in the sights of the surging, debris-filled water, and it swept through the town during peak tourist season. Many more lives would have been lost if not for the early morning efforts of Stephen Gillette, who was collecting trash from the Lawn Lake trailhead when he saw and heard the coming catastrophe. He alerted park rangers, who sounded the alarm to town officials. As Roaring River widened, it completely inundated Estes Park's main thoroughfare of Elkhorn Avenue, flooding businesses, hotels, and restaurants, causing an estimated $30 million in damages. Many of the businesses never returned.

In the early 1900s, Lawn Lake dam had been built with the best of intentions as a means of providing irrigation water storage for farmers in the Loveland area. However, over the course of almost eighty years, the water had turned from a source of sustenance into a source of destruction, largely due to neglect and lack of regular maintenance of the dam.

As a result of this disaster, three other man-made dams located on Bluebird, Pear, and Sandbeach Lakes—situated in the Wild Basin area northwest of Allenspark, at the headwaters of South St. Vrain Creek—were torn down. They had served the City of Longmont and irrigation ditch companies in the Greater St. Vrain Valley.

Thirty-seven years after the Big Thompson Flood, in the fall of 2013, Colorado witnessed yet another flood that in its size and scope made the 1976 Big Thompson and the 1982 Lawn Lake floods pale in comparison.

As we officially ended the 2013 summer season, the mountains and Front Range communities in northern Colorado experienced several days of ever-increasing torrential rain such as hadn't been seen in years. The moisture was most welcome at first. Colorado had been suffering through a multiyear drought statewide, bringing back vivid images of the Dust Bowl years, especially in the southeastern corner of the state.

This time on September 11, not only the Big Thompson River but the Roaring River, North and South St. Vrain, Cache la Poudre, and lesser rivers and streams—all with headwaters originating high in the Colorado Rockies in Rocky Mountain National Park—became raging torrents of water, eventually emptying into the North and South Platte Rivers. Swollen and laden with debris, the waters headed east, carving newer and wider channels as they overflowed onto farmland and into rural towns and communities, and crossing the eastern plains into neighboring Nebraska and Kansas.

Three earthen dams gave way in the foothills between Lyons and Pinewood Springs, northwest of Longmont, sending thousands of gallons of water, sediment, and huge rocks into the St. Vrain River. As the river

Remnants of State Highway 34 ravaged by floodwaters at the mouth of Big Thompson Canyon seen here on Sept. 17, 2013. It brought eerie comparisons to the flood of 37 years ago in July 1976 where 144 lives were lost. One hopeful note—this time around the syphon pipeline remained intact. (Jenny Sparks, photographer, Loveland Reporter-Herald)

rushed through the canyon, it washed away massive sections of U.S. Highway 36 and roared down into Lyons, causing great damage. U.S. Highway 34 up the Big Thompson was completely submerged and washed away again.

Interstate 25 from south of Longmont north to the Wyoming state line, and Interstate 70 from east of Denver to the Kansas border, were closed for many hours as officials waited for water levels to subside. Communications, though vastly improved with twenty-first century capabilities, were significantly hampered due to downed telephone and telecommunications towers, damaged electric grids, and completely inundated roads and bridges in a large part of the state.

Only National Guard helicopters transporting emergency search and rescue personnel were able to get into the rugged mountain areas or to the extensive farm and ranch lands on the northeastern plains. Television news helicopters fed dramatic images of flooded farm fields, stranded

Longmont Times-Call *front-page flood coverage in the immediate aftermath told the story in words and pictures giving initial damage assessments. Citizens and communities along the Front Range, foothills, and mountain towns pulled together to help each other.*

people, and livestock in rural communities, cut off from the rest of the state. One compelling image of a lone horse standing in the corner of a corral as waters from the South Platte rushed by, completely encircling him, came to symbolize the isolation and helplessness Colorado's citizens were feeling.

When the flood waters finally subsided, destroyed homes, railroad tracks, state and interstate highways, county roads, and bridges throughout northern Colorado were left in their wake.

Ten people lost their lives. Tragic as this loss of life was, compared to the 1976 flood, it was truly a miracle more lives were not lost. In 1976 the flood came at the peak of tourist season, so a large number of campers were in the campgrounds of the Big Thompson Canyon and the mountain towns of Glen Haven and Drake with no means of escape, but in 2013 the tourist season was over and school was back in session.

We were very fortunate in receiving badly needed assistance from the men and women of the Colorado National Guard, as well as National Guard units from Utah, Wyoming, and other surrounding states. They rescued stranded flood victims and constructed temporary roads and bridges before winter set in.

Families, friends, neighbors, and total strangers aided the people hardest hit in the small mountain communities, Front Range towns, and eastern rural farms and ranches—a testament to Colorado's long-standing community spirit.

Chapter Twenty-Nine

ADJUSTING THE RUDDER AND STEERING OPERATIONS

THE START OF 1977 PROMISED TO BE MOST CHALLENGING as we took on a rough week with considerable personnel turnover in the Longmont newsroom.

Ruth and I had long been aware that our news product was in a real rut. We also realized we were working with a limited number of experienced operating executives that included Tom Reeves, Blaine Hayes, Bob Cook, and Dan Schrader. However, business had been very good, and about eighty-five percent of the operation was running quite well.

Both daily newspapers were within a few miles of towns with major public universities and access to journalism school graduates. This allowed us to carry out an energetic internship program at each paper with the University of Colorado in Boulder feeding the *Times-Call* and Colorado State University in Fort Collins supplying the *Reporter-Herald* with sharp and talented young journalists.

Over the years we had a number of outstanding editors and reporters who served us well. Some would go on to successful careers in major metropolitan papers throughout the country. We also employed local people in our operations, helping to boost the economies in each community and bringing together a unique group of associates with distinctively diverse backgrounds, experience, and skills.

One day in late January, as a luncheon meeting was drawing to a close, Blaine Hayes, production manager, left for a 4 p.m. doctor's appointment. He learned his blood had a tremendously high white cell count. The following day, Blaine and his wife, Alyce, were visibly shaken by the news of his test results. By late afternoon the following day we heard a rumble from the production department that printing of the *Roundhouse* edition, a *Times-Call* monthly publication, had been overlooked. The pages were finally recovered, and press work was completed the following day. My fears concerning a substantial lack of depth and real understanding in production oversight were being realized. The health emergency we had on our hands highlighted these weaknesses.

By mid-February, we had made some major management changes, and it was turning into an excellent time. The *Times-Call* newsroom was running much smoother under Lee Spaulding's direction as city editor, and the *Reporter-Herald* was making real progress in circulation. We also were making headway with some scheduling and other operations reorganization.

Ruthann now held a master's degree in journalism with a business emphasis from the University of Wisconsin-Madison. In 1977 she was named state political editor to cover the state legislature along with other responsibilities for the Lehman papers. She was doing a fine job in the area coverage and during that summer she worked for the Associated Press in Denver. She worked odd hours, but it offered her an excellent chance to learn the inside of the newswire world. There certainly was no shortage of things to be done.

Dean, who had been studying very hard and making progress in law school, was also working hard on a circulation training manual for the papers. He got along so well in the plant with the staff. It was great having him work side by side with us.

Although business was good, I thought circulation could be better. We just weren't showing the gains equivalent to the steadily increasing populations of the communities we served.

As July 1977 drew to a close, I realized how extremely fortunate we were, keenly aware that we had blessings beyond our ability to recognize or count. More important than anything else was my ability to maintain an even temper and a balanced approach. It wasn't easy, but a buoyant personality added so much to keeping the ship on a steady course, even in choppy waters. Although there continued to be many things giving cause for anger and concern, they were outweighed by a commitment to see the bigger picture and maintain a positive atmosphere, because it could become contagious. More importantly, a positive attitude was the key to survival.

Another key to survival, Ruth and I discovered, was in taking brief vacations from work. Our mountain home on Taylor Mountain near Allenspark provided just the right amount of rustic living and brisk mountain air to distract us from our hectic business lives.

One such interlude came on a bright day in late August when we visited another world in a three-mile walk up to Jim's Grove en route to Longs Peak, one of Colorado's 54 mountains with heights exceeding 14,000 feet. As we passed above timberline, the view widened out into one of nature's greatest panoramas. Longs Peak, Mt. Meeker, and Mt. Lady Washington, each displaying their unique personalities, showcased the glistening rock strata in Mt. Meeker, contrasting with the sheer rock verticals of Longs Peak. The weather was exceptional, although by nighttime a heavy rain began to fall over the entire area.

We were introduced to names such as Goblin's Trail, used primarily by park rangers, and the Boulder Fields, located just below the summit of Longs Peak, which gave us a distinct new perception of rock climbing. We hoped someday to top this grand mountain, but this particular day we proceeded down to Chasm Lake at the foot of Longs Peak for a most memorable and satisfying day.

By 1978 the size of our business and its growth potential had caught up with us, and we were immersed within a machine that didn't seem to stop. One day, following much down thinking about operations and the problems we were confronting, we had a remarkable 2:30 to 10:30 p.m. meeting with Tom Reeves where we laid out the problems and concentrated on some solutions.

The following day, Reeves looked like a new man, and we felt like new people with a better course for steering into the wind and gales of operations. That week we had the best editorial board meeting we'd had in months, everything just clicked into place at an amazing pace. By the weekend we were thinking positively but feeling the fatigue.

Ruthann returned to cover the state legislature, which began with a tumultuous day as Gov. Dick Lamm declared and then un-declared a Broncos state holiday after being informed he didn't have the authority to do this.

I took a stab at interviewing John Rawlings, an advertising sales rep, about becoming my administrative assistant. We sure needed the help— we were trying to do too much with too little staff. He was to give me an answer by Monday. I felt better regardless of his decision, since I knew he needed to broaden his grasp of operations. I could not have imagined a better course of action for his development. In the end, Rob Simons took on the responsibilities as my new assistant and promotion manager. He had a good mind, and I saw a glimmer of genius in this large and kindly man.

In the midst of great stirrings regarding remodeling in the two daily plants, Loveland was about to rearrange and move many departments around, and Longmont needed substantial modification in its newsroom. We had to be ready to march further into the electronic age with the arrival of new computer systems on April 1. The bulk of the impact would be felt in Loveland, but it had great secondary waves for Longmont, too. Meanwhile, our machinery was treating us well. What a crazy business, but very habit forming.

On February 1, 1978, Tom Reeves really surprised me with a call wishing me "Happy 21st anniversary at the newspapers." The significance of the date had completely eluded me, and I hurried to tell Ruth. Truly, it had been an amazing twenty-one-year journey with continuously new challenges. There was never a chance to rest upon the oars because of always changing conditions. We were busier than ever.

Indeed, we still had problems that involved lots of additional people, both inside and outside, and lots more dollars. Our business and the world had become more complicated, and there rarely were simple problems or solutions anymore. Things were more involved, and it took us longer to make changes.

However, if I had it to do all over, I would rush to do the same things again. It didn't seem like twenty-one years. In many ways, it seemed only yesterday. All the ghosts, good and bad, filled the rooms of my mind as I reflected.

On the eve of the centennial convention of the Colorado Press Association in mid-February, we were in our usual dithers. The volume of news, threatened competition, and operational hurdles ran unabated toward some unforeseen goal. But I was very pleased that both Ruthann and Dean were at the Colorado Press convention. Both were great newspaper people and I would match them against anyone I knew.

As we focused on final planning for a major overhaul of the news and production areas at both papers, we were also looking at some really big price items. The advertising and news computer systems, the circulation insert equipment, and more press units all required attention. Somewhere on the timescale was the need to enlarge the Longmont plant as well. And ever present was our Denver real estate division that consumed so much of our time.

We were also looking at competition. In Loveland a man started a "shopper," a free distribution newspaper. In Longmont, a Sunday weekly called *The Ledger* was going into its third week as of February 1, 1978. We had mounted a fierce opposition, but this competitor was far from knocked out.

Although business was pretty good, I thought *Times-Call* sales had slipped down during the previous month. We still were ahead, but in those days of inflation, you had to be a *long* way ahead.

On top of everything else, we had made a pass at ownership of another daily paper, this one called the *Cañon City Daily Record*. We were awaiting word from the owners, the Hardy family.

Ruthann, our total newspaperwoman, was in the closing hours of the General Assembly. How proud we were of her representation of our newspapers and the industry in general. She was perceptive, ring-wise, and, despite a tough exterior, a person with a deep, delightful sense of humor. It was truly a rewarding and rich experience to be associated with her.

Chapter Thirty

ARSONIST

ON APRIL 20, 1978, I TOOK LEE SPAULDING, *Times-Call* city editor, to supper at the Imperial Hotel where we had a great visit as we reviewed our problems and our successes. The evening ended with him talking to a fire department officer on a negotiation regarding the sad state of affairs of our fire department, especially in light of a number of recent arson fires.

The following week, I had a meeting with two fire department officers on the same subject. I also called the mayor and discussed the possibility of developing a volunteer force in cooperation with the paid department. To my surprise, Mayor E. George Patterson Jr. totally endorsed our efforts and asked me to continue advocating for a volunteer force, with his blessings.

The fire department faced an unprecedented challenge at this time. Lewellen's Funeral Home still smelled from the damage wrought by an arsonist's latest handiwork. Howe Mortuary wasn't yet operational following a bombing there. The owners of Ahlberg Funeral Chapel, the *Times-Call's* next-door neighbor, felt their location was likely next. Longmont was troubled with a rampant arsonist who (off the record) was confirmed as a necrophiliac after setting seven fires at Howe Mortuary and leaving one embalmed female somewhat the worse for wear. At a luncheon with the director of safety and the chief of detective operations, Calvin Case, we learned they felt that a very disturbed individual was on the loose in the community.

We had night patrols in the central area of town, but the perpetrator was still at large. I tried to call the sole Longmont detective assigned to the case, to tell him of an idea I had been forming, but he was out. I wanted a silent, secret alarm in Ahlberg's so the police and those businesses in the immediate vicinity would know when the arsonist was about to strike again. It seemed so obvious that the police could not be everywhere in going after the arsonist; a trap had to be set to bring him out in the open.

I proceeded on my own to hire a night security guard and stationed him on the roof patio deck of the *Times-Call* building. This provided a perfect vantage point for keeping watch on the alleys and general areas where the arsonist had been wreaking havoc.

Eventually the arsonist was caught when the security guard spotted him and notified the police. In the end, the man was determined to be mentally ill and sentenced to the Colorado State Mental Hospital in Pueblo, where he died several years later.

Chapter Thirty-One

COMPETITION

WORD CARRIED IN BY BILL JOHNSON, vice president of sales and marketing, that an 83-acre shopping center was about to be developed just across State Highway 66, north of Longmont, was of great importance to the wallet.

J. C. Penney was an acknowledged tenant, along with three other major occupants. A recheck confirmed that another shopping center was also on the drawing board, this one across from the new fairgrounds southwest of town. All of this added up to us needing to produce either a Sunday newspaper or a Sunday shopper. We had much analysis and planning to do before making the decision to either add another daily publication or go with a weekly shopper. In the final analysis we did both. We began publishing a Sunday paper and we added a mid-week shopper, distributed to all addresses in the St. Vrain Valley.

The anticipated computer system was to begin a new era for us. The Loveland news staff moved entirely onto electronic terminals. Longmont really was the catching station for Loveland production, but within eighteen months both Loveland and Longmont would be directly wired to mainframe computers, speeding up the entire advertising, news, and production operations.

Blaine Hayes, our production manager, was out after suffering a heart attack. But the race continued at a relentless pace. We never should have expected it would slow down. The challenge was to come up to speed and then cruise along with the new pace.

We completed the annual corporate meetings to summarize a most remarkable year of growth. In many ways, we had an extraordinary business and two great communities in Longmont and Loveland. Perhaps Ruth and I were the only people in our top management who fully appreciated our deep problems and our shortcomings. We knew we still did not have the full management team or the most effective approach. There would be many miles to travel before we did.

The Thursday, June 29, 1978, edition of *The Ledger* was reportedly the last of this effort in competition. *The Ledger* had begun with 14,000 Sunday delivery in February. In the last five weeks of this publication, it had also put out a Thursday edition. We studied their volume and were convinced they were losing hundreds of dollars on each edition. We knew it could not last, but we had known the same about other efforts. Bill Johnson told me this was the sixteenth competitive publication that had sought to operate against us since he came to Longmont in 1968. We believed that competitive publications lost more than $250,000 in proving and reproving that the market just was not sufficient (or large enough) to support two competitive publications.

Still, basically, we did not sleep. We followed up with each advertiser with a stronger sales message and showed how we were a better investment. Advertisers do not place ads because they like a publication or its publisher. They spend advertising dollars to get results for their businesses.

One of the basic tenets of our business was to never ignore competition, regardless of how small. We acted and spurred on the staff toward greater sales efforts. A competitor soon discovered there was no repeating base. They were forever plowing new ground that they knew would erode before another edition. Naturally, we did not succeed with every advertiser, but we were able to move the advertisers who were poor credit risks to the competitor. After a while, the competitor was filled with poor accounts that did not pay, and eventually had to shutter their doors.

In previous years one of our greatest challenges had been Bill Roberts, a former *Times-Call* advertising manager who sold his advertising with continuing contracts. After he left, it became necessary for us to present our greatest sales efforts as his contracts expired. Eventually his excellent initial financing was extended to the advertisers. After leaving the *Times-Call* Roberts and his wife, Agnes, along with a few shareholders, started up a weekly called *The Scene*, but by November 1975, they sold out.

Fatigue, discouragement, and a parched advertising desert all contributed to an impossible environment for competing newspapers. To succeed, a competitor had to excel in news, advertising, production, circulation, and business operations—a hefty challenge.

An early fall swept across the landscape in August 1978, bringing relief from the summer heat. The news cycle was tedious, which set the stage for more exciting moments waiting on the wings of time. I felt the Carter administration couldn't stumble on much longer without meeting an unexpected wall.

Carl Hilliard's timely column "Capitol Close Up" of September 8, 1978, stirred many memories about former U.S. Sen. Eugene Milliken during the period of 1948 through 1950:

> *The time is 1950.*
>
> *U.S. Sen. Eugene Milliken, R-Colo., is a worried man.*
>
> *Republicans had suffered heavy losses in the Democratic landslide of 1948. The Colorado GOP was beset with rivalries and friction and lacked direction and leadership.*
>
> *Milliken himself had a health problem. Two healthy and popular Democrats, Gov. Lee Knous and Congressman John Carroll, were ready to take him on for the Senate.*
>
> *But Milliken turned political liabilities around and won re-election, sweeping Republican candidates into office with him.*
>
> *A fascinating account of how he did that is in a book called "Readings in Colorado Government and Politics," published in 1967 by the University of Colorado, co-authored by Curtis Martin and Wallace Stealey.*
>
> *Stealey, a former legislative aide to Gov. Richard Lamm, is now campaign manager for State Sen. Ray Kogovsek in his quest for Congress in the 3rd District.*
>
> *One chapter is called "Mr. Republican's Greatest Victory." It is by Cyrus C. Wells, who some Republicans will recall was involved in Republican organizational politics from 1960 through the early 1970s. He served for a time as state party secretary.*
>
> *Wells' chapter about Milliken and his 1950 campaign is admittedly worshipful of the late senator, but it points up parallel situations today in both parties, but probably more among Republicans.*

And any candidate, who feels the odds are against his election, or re-election, should read Wells' account of what happened.

Republican Party friction was caused by previous primaries and poor losers. Old guard members were reluctant to accept new party organizations and political ideas.

Milliken ignored criticism about new blood in the party, accepted new ideas and smoothed over some ruffled feelings.

Then, disaster.

Ralph C. Carr, the party nominee for governor, died after the primary. GOP officials hurriedly met in Colorado Springs and picked Carr's successor, an obscure Gunnison legislator and cattleman named Dan Thornton.

Despite Thornton's tendency to be a political maverick, Milliken managed to work with him during the campaign.

Without going into Wells' blow-by-blow account of how Milliken turned the campaign around, here are five major factors involved in that achievement.

They were:
- *Milliken's hard-hitting and logical articulation of the issues.*
- *His seizing and maintaining the offensive.*
- *His willingness to study opposition statements and to carefully prepare replies.*
- *His witty ridicule of the bevy of outside speakers—including Vice President Alben W. Barkley—to campaign for his eventual opponent, John Carroll.*
- *The combined product of a keen mind and a sharp sense of humor.*

Jack Fitzpatrick, dean of the statehouse press corps and long-time reporter for radio station KHOW in Denver, recalls an example of Milliken's ability to bulldoze people into action.

Milliken was addressing a group of Republican dowagers at the Brown Palace at the beginning of the campaign. At one point in Milliken's speech, Fitzpatrick recalls the tall, blustering U.S. senator as saying:

> *"We've got to get off our ass and ring doorbells—and I mean what I say. We've got to get off our ass."*
>
> *While the stately but startled ladies were recovering from that outburst, reporters were hurrying to telephones to dictate the latest in a series of good stories about a good political campaign.*
>
> *Statewide, Milliken won by 29,282 votes—and even carried Denver, a Democratic stronghold, by 541 votes. He lost in only 14 of Colorado's 63 counties.*
>
> *Thornton beat Walter Johnson by 23,456 votes. Gordon Allott was elected lieutenant governor; Wellington "Duke" Dunbar was elected attorney general and Early Ewing nipped Myron McGinley for state treasurer.*

Basically Ruth and I agreed with the column, but we questioned Jack Fitzpatrick's recollection of the language. Our recollection was that Senator Milliken got across the idea without the language. He was a forceful man with tremendous wit and wisdom who had an incredible grasp of government and the problems of his time.

Chapter Thirty-Two

OUR TWO-FRONT WAR

CONTINUOUSLY AT THE EDGE OF OUR CONSCIOUSNESS was the Denver real estate. It represented many, many hours of work and trips to Denver, and I knew it was a gamble, but down deep I felt good about it. Ted Sievert, Colorado chief engineer of buildings for Mountain Bell (formerly Mountain States Telephone & Telegraph), believed we were in a blighted area in a declining neighborhood and had moved employees out of the building. I argued against this, but he still did not want to move people back into the 18th Avenue location.

As preparations were under way for a Mountain Bell removal from the 18th Avenue complex on September 15, 1979, we got a complete "complex" over this property—183,000 square feet of real estate, which indeed justified the term *complex*. A block and a half was not to be taken lightly. It was a chunk of our hometown, Denver. Indeed we were on the brink of rare and challenging real estate adventures, which I hoped would not lead us into a financial crisis.

We met on a takeover plan that would be directed toward various degrees of mothballing the buildings. If necessary we would see this project through to a real success. Central Denver was a booming place. The experts said that to replace these structures on the market would cost $7 million, including the land.

We marched on with a quiet faith and a steadfast determination. We expected to emerge all right, but were prepared to fall back many yards before regrouping for the final, successful surge as we found ourselves in the midst of a two-front war: the burgeoning newspaper world and one-and-one-half blocks of Denver real estate. The German general staff warned of a major two-front war; I now understood their philosophy.

We left other demanding situations and "made the time" for management matters on the 18th Avenue complex. I recall spending an entire day in Denver working on this, making much progress. There is nothing like personally getting close to a series of problems. In building matters, it is of particular importance to go and take a look.

Back at the newspaper, a department head meeting revealed that employees seemed to be dealing well with the new computer system, which had gone online June 23 in Loveland. Meanwhile, we had purchased the *Frederick Farmer and Miner* and the *Erie Echo* weekly newspapers, each in small rural towns southeast of Longmont. We would take over fully on September 15.

There never was a dull moment. I am not totally sure why we kept going at the pace we did, but I was also unsure of how we would have slowed down. There is an old saying that it is a great life, if you don't weaken. We certainly were proving it.

Business was unbelievably good. Yet, with the pressures on the dollar and the poor national leadership, I wondered how long the real good times could continue. Bit by bit, we appeared to be gathering the best staff in the history of the newspapers. Indeed, times were changing.

I asked myself if experience and wisdom made up for the loss of physical drive and stamina. As growth and prosperity filled our sails, we tended to boldly solve some problems with dollars we never would have spent in earlier years. Were we spending because of a concern there was no tomorrow or because ahead was a greater tomorrow? Time would tell, and the answers would come later.

Life was amazing and challenging in innumerable ways as we progressed in a sea of tension. The basic health chart of our newspaper businesses perked along in a most vigorous fashion, yet we found ample areas for tension built upon worries. We lived in a world of haste, but in many business problems, the pace could not remotely have kept up with expectations. For example, remodeling was needed in the production area at the *Times-Call* to accommodate equipment, both old and new. Instead, we needed a calm approach at the very time we were rushing toward an unobtainable goal. While most of the proposals from managers to grow the business were needed, they had to realize we must remain solvent and that everything could not be accomplished at once.

Blaine Hayes was one of the few managers with the total grasp of this. He told me on several occasions technology was changing so rapidly that the equipment and software to run it were practically obsolete by the time they arrived for installation.

Outside influences received the credit for rush, rush. Actually, the deep, penetrating pressures to continue modernizing production procedures and expand the business were applied only from the inside. Although the newspaper business inherently is very fast, the real estate business is slow, with much of it based on the passage of generations and eventual funerals. We needed to pace ourselves and wait for developments on our purchase proposals for other newspapers as well as the sale of the 18th Avenue building in Denver.

Chapter Thirty-Three

EXPANSION TO THE SOUTH— CAÑON CITY

IN THOSE BUSY TIMES OF 1978, Ruth and I still hoped to get away for a brief vacation, but throughout the summer department heads either had illnesses or vacations, so there was no way. Our new weeklies, the *Erie Echo* and the *Frederick Farmer and Miner* experienced painful, but not hazardous, births.

With unexpected suddenness in October, the Cañon City newspaper proposal abruptly broke open. Tom Reeves reached us by telephone in Santa Fe, and by the next day, Ruth and I were en route to Cañon City.

I met Dave Hardy on Monday, October 9, and reopened the negotiations. He had sugar plums dancing in his head. He wanted quite a lot for a very sick animal, but we felt it was a great opportunity.

We hurried home to Longmont and spent several hours in profound thought, figuring the countless avenues available to us with Cañon City. Although we were rather discouraged by the extremely high interest rates, we also were cautiously hopeful. Fortunately, the two dailies and three weeklies were all perking along well, and business was good.

By late October, as the world was spinning rapidly, we moved into deep negotiations in Cañon City while at the same time facing the 1978 election windup and upcoming holidays.

The previous week we had been in Chicago for the Inland convention. We left the convention early so I could attend a three-day meeting of the University of Denver Alumni Board. As the first vice president, I was headed forward to the board presidency. Privately I was having second thoughts that perhaps the best thing would be for me not to be nominated for board president.

"Operation CC" (Cañon City) had forced us to reexamine our entire internal organization. We needed to get ownership into the hands of our key management associates. We long had talked about this plan. We wanted them to work more closely with Ruthann and Dean during our absence—such as business trips, vacations, and eventually as they began taking over various aspects of management.

On November 8, 1978, we purchased the *Cañon City Daily Record*. I was a little numb. Ruthann reported she was just going to sit on the floor and think. We gave the word to Dean's answering machine. This troubled, sad, yet very exciting, community needed a really good newspaper. I knew we could do it.

Ruth and I were in one of the funniest negotiating sessions as the project moved into the final rounds. Our attorney, Frank King, made one proud of the legal profession. I silently prayed for God to bless our efforts and give us the strength of a dozen people. The deal for the 6,942-circulation newspaper involved a long 20-year payout. The sellers, the Hardy family, also insisted on a few fancy tax gimmicks. We had some doubts, but they were determined to proceed with those provisions. It certainly took optimists to make a deal like this.

The agreements were finalized on November 17, and we jointly announced the *Daily Times-Call* purchase of the *Cañon City Daily Record*, with actual takeover of operations to begin November 30. It had been a long, intense road to this point. Now, the real work would begin, and only time would tell whether this was good for Fremont County as well as for us.

The Cañon City Daily Record, located southwest of Colorado Springs, was founded by Dr. Isaac E. Thayer in February 1875, just four years after the *Times-Call* in Longmont. Called the *Cañon City Weekly Avalanche* by April 1878, the name was later changed to the *Fremont County Record*.

By 1895, it was called the *Weekly Cañon City Record* and was purchased by Guy U. Hardy, who served seven terms as a U.S. congressman and was responsible for federal action giving the Royal Gorge Bridge and park area to Cañon City. He also built the two-story Record Building in 1901 at 521 Main Street, with a grocery store sharing the ground floor. On July 16, 1906, the *Weekly Record* became the *Cañon City Daily Record* and remains that to this day.

Upon the death of Guy Hardy in 1947, his son Don became the publisher. In June 1965 Don was succeeded by his son David, who became the third generation to publish the family newspaper.

Looking west on Main Street the Cañon City Daily Record *is at right, second building from the corner. Operating as the eyes and ears of Cañon City, Florence, Penrose, and Fremont and Custer Counties since before Colorado became a state, the newspaper has documented the area's colorful stories, successes and sorrows, people, places, and events from 1875 through 2016. Spanning the last quarter of the nineteenth, all of the twentieth, and almost a quarter of the twenty-first centuries, 141 years of continuous coverage is a lot of history.*

In 1968 a three-year major conversion project began, which took the *Record* from hot lead metal to the cold type production process, and a new three-unit Goss Community press was installed to replace an aging flatbed press. The *Record* expanded into the remaining half of the first floor, previously occupied by an appliance store, and in the early 1970s, a fourth unit was added to the press.

The area in and around Cañon City was home to a number of ranches, farms, and fruit orchards, thanks to the mild year-round climate. But the leading industries that employed the most people were mining and the Territorial Prison, or "Old Max", that opened in 1871. A new federal penitentiary Administrative Maximum Penitentiary (ADX), or "Super Max", opened in November 1994. At the time, the county was already home to nine prisons and more would follow.

In the early 1950s, uranium was discovered thirty-five miles northwest of the town. Within a year a bill was approved by the U.S. House of Representatives allowing uranium mining on public lands, bringing Colorado into a three-state partnership with New Mexico and Utah. Four years later, a uranium pilot mill was built south of Cañon City by Cotter Corporation. Before the decade was out, Cotter was producing 200 tons of ore a day.

In the 1960s, the mill was a full-scale uranium operation supplying foreign as well as domestic users. By the early 1970s, the mill would be receiving, in open rail cars, thousands of tons of radioactive residue tailings from the Manhattan Project.

In 1974 Commonwealth Edison Company of Chicago bought Cotter, which at the time had a payroll of 81 persons. By 1978 the mill was processing 400 tons of ore per day with a workforce of 148, second only to the state prisons in Cañon City as principal employers of the area.

I took on the added challenges and responsibilities as president and publisher of the Royal Gorge Publishing Company and found myself eager and full of enthusiasm. Perhaps I dreamed big dreams, and those about me never would experience placid, peaceful times, but it was my destiny to challenge, drive, and urge a most skillful group of associates toward greater accomplishments and goals. My spare moments were filled with the most exciting thoughts of how we could serve this community and be a positive influence on its future.

John "Stump" Witcher, former Fremont County District Attorney and friend and colleague from the 1940s and '50s, was still in town and most supportive of our efforts as the new owners of the *Daily Record*. It felt good to have some local support as the new owners of the newspaper.

The Longmont and Loveland newspapers needed constant care with expanding challenges and obstacles of their own. Our hands were busy. Our feet were busy. Would we have it any differently? Together, we marched into new chapters. If we could serve the many thousands of people in our audiences, we would have done our best for civilization in our time and place. Once again, I prayed for God to bless our efforts and multiply our strength.

So many improvements were needed at a newspaper property that had been largely neglected for three generations. The grandfather, Guy U. Hardy, had been a member of Congress for fourteen years, and this was his true interest. His son Don was a world traveler and extremely active in the National Newspaper Association. The grandson Dave was never truly interested in being a newspaperman. However, had the Hardy's put the newspaper and its business first, we would not have been there. And, in turn, we would not have been at the Longmont National Bank borrowing $100,000 (a portion of the sales price) at 10¼ percent interest.

Still business was good. The previous month Longmont and Loveland had done half a million dollars in volume. However, it certainly would have been far easier had the Cañon City takeover been January 1, instead of November 30.

The Cañon City Daily Record *had been serving the Upper Arkansas River Valley since 1875. In addition to having one of the highest circulation penetrations in this area of the country, in 1983 (when this photo was taken), the plant produced a wide variety of commercial print products.*

A warming trend was most welcome after a very heavy dose of winter, but the U.S. and world economic pattern looked a little bleak as we entered 1979. Many clouds were on the horizon. America was going through a down period. President Carter went from one crisis to another, usually ending up on the lower side of coming out ahead. The inflation threat existed everywhere, yet we were either in or on the brink of a recession. Unquestionably, we were in the midst of a great turnaround. What was commonly referred to as *future* shock was *here* and *now!*

Cañon City was a marvelous test that just didn't quit. Gaining the upper hand in managing and turning around a business that had been in decline for quite some time with a staff and a community largely reluctant to change and easily satisfied with the status quo provided unending challenges.

Tom Reeves had been there a week, and we talked at least twice a day in long, intense conversations, making many decisions. At one point Tom had to recall 3,000 copies of the paper to get a page remade due to a dangerous story about possible charges against a geriatric home operator. Tom also reported we had built an additional $90,000 in increased personnel costs into Cañon City.

The renovating process began by completely remodeling the 4,000-square-foot warehouse at 920 Royal Gorge Boulevard with the installation of a new, very heavy concrete floor for the storage of newsprint rolls.

In Longmont we were busy covering and reporting on major disruption over the 4-to-3 vote to remove School Superintendent Dr. John McKenna, and the City Council was completely up in the air over two competing shopping center sites.

As Ruth and I prepared to leave for Chicago February 17, 1979, to attend the Inland Daily Press Association meeting, we found ourselves searching for an accounting head to replace Dan Schrader in Longmont and an editor/general manager for Cañon City. Tom Reeves, who was very good at budgeting, was already in Chicago heading the Inland Cost and Revenue Study, a role he superbly filled.

By mid-March I had hired Doug Miles, a career newspaperman, as editor and general manager of the *Daily Record*. Ruthann was rightfully displeased with me because she was not included in the interview process. Previously she had been a most helpful and accurate member of a selection committee. It was one of those management decisions that had to be made before an opportunity got away. In turn, I was hopeful Ruthann would go ahead with an interview of her own and reach some most worthwhile understandings before Miles reported the following Monday for work.

As an old manager, I only could say that if Doug Miles was the success I believed he would be, then all would be okay. If he was a failure, my name would be mud, and I would have made what some predicted would be "a two-year mistake."

We certainly had a basketful of management problems. We also had some excellent assistants, but we needed to use them more effectively. We were at a major turning point in the operation of our companies. I felt the road ahead would become a broadened highway with a much smoother surface with the right personnel, but wrong personnel decisions could send us down a rocky road and give us some very rough going. At the time I was optimistic because I believed we were getting the right people for the challenges ahead—and there would be many.

Ironically, less than a month after Miles came on board, one of America's worst nuclear accidents occurred inside the Three Mile Island nuclear plant in Pennsylvania on March 28, prompting the "No Nukes" movement. Many states began rationing gas, and thousands protested for safer fuel sources.

There would be more than twenty years of almost daily coverage of the Cotter Corporation, with investigations by the U.S. Environmental Protection Agency, Colorado Bureau of Investigation, and state health officials. Lawsuits ultimately would bring an out-of-court settlement with a clean-up plan in December 1987, but that would not be the end of this tale. By the 1990s the case was appealed and civil suits were filed by sixteen residents known as the Dodge group. The case languished without a definitive decision until July 2001, when the plaintiffs were awarded slightly more than $16 million in damages, an amount that jumped to $43.5 million with interest. Cotter appealed but was required to bond the full amount of damages first.

In February 2002, after Cotter announced it would receive 270,000 tons of waste from a designated Superfund site in Maywood, N.J., Gov. Bill Owens quickly signed an emergency bill into law, requiring an environmental assessment and state health department review before any out-of-state radioactive waste could be shipped into Colorado. When the Colorado Department of Public Health and Environment cited Cotter with 16 violations of its license, nearly 40 percent of its workforce was laid off. By July the company was suspended from accepting any more off-site shipments of ore until these violations were addressed.

Our twenty-four years of coverage culminated in October 2002 with the publication of "The Cotter Files—Cotter at a Crossroads." Key administrators, editors, reporters, and photographers from the three daily newspapers contributed to this publication: Ruthann Lehman, who by this time had changed her name to Lauren, was now operations manager of the *Daily Record* and senior vice president of Lehman Communications Corporation; Ken Amundson, assistant to the publisher and project coordinator for the Cotter series; Terri Holloway, general manager; Lee Spaulding, managing editor; Grant Murray, news assistant; and Tamara McCumber, photographer, all of the *Cañon City Daily Record*; B. J. Plasket, Denver bureau reporter for Lehman Communications Corporation; Eric Frankowski, assistant city editor; Travis Pryor, day news editor; Kim Humphreys, consulting editor; Patrick Kramer, chief photographer; and Jeff Haller, photographer, all of the *Longmont Daily Times-Call*; and Jackie Hutchins, local news editor of the *Loveland Daily Reporter-Herald*. The *Daily Record* received Scripps-Howard's top National Journalism Award for environmental reporting for newspapers under 100,000 circulation for the special publication.

Uranium was not the only hot topic of the day. The prison system, still with its penchant for making headlines, began major growth changes in the 1980s. A new maximum security prison was built east of town, with a total of thirteen ancillary places of incarceration constructed, all within close proximity to Cañon City, prompting the Colorado State Patrol to build a regional office on the east edge of town.

The last decade of the twentieth century and the first decade of the twenty-first century would see some of the more notorious criminals of the era relocated to state prisons in Fremont County and the Federal Correctional Complex in Florence.

Suddenly this rural town situated at the western edge of the Arkansas Valley—and deemed the "climate capital of Colorado"—was experiencing a life-changing facelift. As with all life-changing events, not everyone was pleased with the results.

Within a relatively short time, there would be nine correctional facilities operating in Fremont County. The Colorado Territorial Correctional Facility, built in 1871 and the oldest, was situated at the base of a mountain on the western edge of town and housed close to 5,000 inmates in a medium security environment, along with some administrative offices. A community sponsored Museum of Colorado Prisons is located nearby.

Located on a 5,600-acre parcel of land on the east boundary of Cañon City is the East Cañon Correctional Complex, site of one of the three women's correctional facilities in the state. The remaining seven of the county's correctional facilities offered a variety of prisoner programs including a pre-release center and agribusiness projects. By 2016 more than half the jobs in the county would be with or related to the corrections industry.

In the end Doug Miles would manage the *Daily Record* for nine years, leaving in 1988. He had numerous accomplishments to his credit. We adhered strictly to the Inland Press Association's guidelines for a balanced circulation/employee ratio at all of our newspaper properties—a proportion he often surpassed substantially. There would be five general managers succeeding him, each taking their turn at the helm over the course of the following twenty-three years—John Hawkins, Daryl Beall, Bob Helsley, Terri Holloway, and Terry Cochran.

We encouraged managers at all of our properties to act decisively and with a certain degree of autonomy. However, it was requisite that they gain an understanding of the bigger corporate picture and how each division fit into total operations. It also required keeping the lines of communication open and collaborative in approach. Some were more successful than others.

We soon discovered the approximately 300-mile round trip distance between Longmont and Cañon City, while not insurmountable, could present some unusual challenges. This distance was manageable when everything was running smoothly. When it wasn't, it placed additional burdens on Ruth and me and our key corporate managers, taking precious time away from our other principal responsibilities to get operations back on track.

The same situation could present itself at the other divisions, too. However, problems in Loveland or Berthoud, Frederick, or Erie usually surfaced quicker and, being much closer to the center of operations in Longmont, were easier to rectify swiftly.

I had several people tell me over the years that they felt as if they had entered a time warp as they left Colorado Springs and headed southwest into Cañon City. They felt like they were going back fifty years in time. One employee who lived in Cañon City referred to it as "the town time forgot." While this had not occurred to me, in retrospect I can see how one would acquire these impressions.

For many years, Cañon City remained quite remote, with a unique character. One of our greatest challenges was getting businesses and people who bore grudges against one another, sometimes going back several generations, to advertise side by side in the paper. Similar to managing the Hatfields and McCoys, it was a constant mediation process.

I remember there was a city councilman in Cañon City who liked to come in and bully the news staff. When we arrived one day, he literally had the staff hiding behind their pencils at their desks. He was having a tantrum. Well, he had one too many tantrums, because he ran into Ruth, who happened to be in the office, and she threw him out. Ruth could be outspoken. She was Scotch-Irish and not afraid of a good fight. The councilman said he was going to get a lawyer. Ruth told him, "You had better get a good one." He never gave us any more trouble after that. We laughed about that many times over the years.

By the spring of 1979 business was on the downturn as we were in a most severe time of recession and inflation. Even if we sold the advertising, we had trouble collecting payment. If I learned anything from this period, it was to welcome and appreciate the good times.

In April Ruth and I took a 2½-week vacation trip to Egypt with the Denver Art Museum associates. The Mideast was another world. At one point I became separated from Ruth and ended up on quite an adventure aboard a camel traveling with my guide in the sweltering heat in and around the pyramids. When he took me inside one of the larger pyramids for a tour at first the coolness was most inviting, but soon I was overtaken by the substantial lack of oxygen and became most anxious to get back outside. I determined I could deal with the heat, but there was no relief for lack of air. Ruth reported having had an equally interesting day, although the specific details now elude me. We exchanged stories after we eventually were reunited following our day of discovery. Unfortunately, it could be a hostile atmosphere for one's health. Ruth stayed well, except for a slight ankle sprain. She and I were of the very few who did not experience serious illness on the trip.

I came to the conclusion the best thing about a vacation trip is coming home. It is not that one does not enjoy seeing new sights and sounds and meeting interesting people. Coming home gives one a moment of new overall clarity of vision as one's immediate world comes back into focus.

Upon our return we found many of our major tasks still with us—the largest being that hunk of real estate in Denver. We faced a difficult time—the now-vacant building, the security, the engineering, and the real estate agents—all presented considerable challenges. Was it a pallid giant or a golden opportunity? Only time and our own efforts would provide the answers. And time was short as each second ticked off the remainder of the Mountain Bell lease due to expire in mid-September.

On a Denver day when our full attention and focus was turned to the 18th Avenue complex, Ruth and I met Vance Hayes, our new manager for the complex, whom we liked very much. A tour of the building showed everything was going along pretty well in ending the lease with the Mountain Bell tenants. Vance and I had lunch, and then I met Bill Prather of Mountain Bell to discuss closeout factors. An hour later I joined Ruth for a conference with Bill Stevens and Fuller & Company Real Estate. It appeared we were on the home stretch in putting together a deal for the sale of the property.

Ruth and I also had our hands full with Cañon City's accounting department. During our trip to Egypt, two additional Goss Urbanite press units were put into operation at the *Times-Call*, bringing the press capacity to fifty-six pages in black, but it was not an easy transition, fraught with many headaches and late press times.

A day to remember was May 23, when the light of day revealed several hidden problems that came home to roost. An inventory error was discovered in Longmont that showed we were down to a one-day supply of 31-inch newsprint. We turned in many directions. A truck was sent to Cañon City for 50 rolls of newsprint. A Crown Zellerbach rail car in Pueblo destined for Cañon City was diverted to Longmont. We had very inexperienced staff in the pressroom. Waste was too high, and accidents happened frequently—torn blankets, press wrecks—all due to human error, tension, and inexperience.

As we began to regroup, cancelling commercial print jobs and special sections; economy and efficiency were to be the hallmarks of the new era. We had been operating the business like there was no end to the boom, but economic indicators were trending downward. Much of the nation was faced with a fuel shortage, and we expected it to strike in Colorado.

We continued to lumber along with the dark cloud of the 18th Avenue complex over us. We had great hopes we could do something good with it, but it was both a demand and a threat. There had been other times, and this was certainly no time to rock the boat. We faced heavy seas and it would require a heavy, strong hand on the tiller. We would weather this storm and be stronger in the long pull, but we faced a long, hard summer.

On a hot summer evening in mid-July 1979, we listened to President Jimmy Carter make his long-awaited energy speech. This deep international problem at last was gaining full recognition in the nation. With it came both inflation and the threat of a recession. Ahead were thought-provoking times. I doubted Carter had the leadership capability to marshal the nation and its people. He and his administration wallowed along as we went from one crisis to the next. The oil-producing nations kept increasing the cost of petroleum, placing us at the mercy of the cartel.

In mid-September I returned from an ANPA (American Newspaper Publishers Association) governmental affairs meeting in Washington, D.C. Our committee had met during many trying times, the Watergate period being the most memorable. This meeting was September 17, 1979, and the urgent topics for discussion were:

Inflation – double digit

Recession – unmistakable and growing worse

Energy – major shortage of all fuels and utter confusion about a major program

Salt II – a major Senate debate with ominous overtones about national defense

Russian troops – 3,000 of them in Cuba, as though they'd never heard of the Monroe Doctrine

Presidential election 1980 – Carter greatly weakened, Ted Kennedy looming, and a mixed field running through the misty moors of GOP politics

Tax laws – Quite up in the air—should we cut or just soak the oil companies for any windfall profits?

Energy replacement vs. environment – Do we go all out and forget possible damage to air and water?

Quality of life – Is it slipping lower each month for many Americans?

The Soviet challenge – In view of America's disarray, isn't it time for the Russian bear to try to apply challenging pressure at numerous points throughout the world?

The Third World – The uncommitted countries, having just finished a convention in Cuba, where are they going? The inflation and skyrocketing fuel costs are bound to have very heavy effects upon them.

America's record prime interest rate – 13 percent and predicted to go higher. If that doesn't stop business development, nothing will. Where is it all going?

Wage and price controls – Are they just around the corner?

Are we slipping into a world depression? – There are many indications that we are bordering on similar conditions that prevailed in 1929.

Summary – These were different and troubled times. In our own businesses, we had seen major unfavorable trend lines developing. We were going to have to do more with less.

We always assume that life goes on, gaining from day to day with business ever expanding. Unfortunately, in those days we were seeing unmistakable symptoms that a change was taking place.

The nation and the world had experienced a most marked inflation. Great concern was expressed by people in all walks of life. Every economic effort was being made to stem the overwhelming tides of inflation. But newspapers also were experiencing the stern, unmistakable symptoms of profitable economic withdrawal.

Advertising lineage was dropping, and bill collections were becoming a major factor in business survival. On all sides, businessmen were facing hard realities. We were going to get through the happy holiday season of 1979 and then look out. A total re-examination would have to be made.

One interesting factor was that business firms that continued advertising and marketing invariably emerged much stronger in the marketplace at the time. The newspaper business was considered a good recession-depression business—if the newspapers watched their own problems.

Chapter Thirty-Four

A BUILDING SALE— MAYBE

BY DECEMBER 27, 1979, Ruth and I had a rare fire drill as we worked desperately in tandem to meet the requirements of a possible sale of the 18th Avenue properties.

The proposed purchasers planned to split the buildings into 900- to 1,800-square-foot units for many, many different tenants. If conditions had been different, we could have done exactly the same thing. However, as a family of owners, Ruth and her sister, Jeanne Land, could not agree on a path forward for keeping the building. Without consensus we were at a stalemate, thus we were in no position to perform these changes ourselves.

With the utmost timed efforts, we completed gathering detailed information to meet the sales requirements for the option to purchase by the SMC Read Corporation of Los Angeles. The most unusual moments arrived with the title insurance commitment, which was incorrect in many areas. Fortunately, Joe Berenbaum (for Ruth's sister, Jeanne) and Hover Lentz (for Ruth) were rapidly acting on the same problems we had noticed.

The Hearth Company, agents for the sale, along with Bill Stevens of Fuller Real Estate, worked intensely pulling everything together. The fun was in the accomplishment of a most complex series of actuaries. Not too many people could have functioned as efficiently as Ruth and I and our secretaries, who operated very well. We set aside newspaper issues and all other problems and just dug into the immediate situation. Quietly we could not help but be pleased at the achievement and teamwork.

It was a momentous occasion when on January 31, 1980, we finally sold the 18th Avenue complex to SMC Read Corporation. It was a four-hour closing, followed by a reception-supper at the Denver Athletic Club.

The following weekend, Ruth and I felt a tremendous letdown over the close of an era. It was too bad that we could not have come together as a family to go forward and get multiple tenants. However, we felt we did well just to get Jeanne through all the steps to the closing. There was no way that the two of us could have continued with our newspaper businesses and taken on the extensive operational responsibilities involved in developing this Denver property.

Unquestionably, there were many dollars to be made in that property assemblage, but it required all owners to be in overall agreement and work well together. In this regard there was no way for a practical avenue of procedure. In hindsight it was all for the best because the risks and the decisions would have required a personal sacrifice that Ruth and I could not make. The sale cleared a great burden from our shoulders. At last we could refocus our full attention on our other business efforts.

Chapter Thirty-Five

1980s—NEW FRONTIER OF EACH DAWNING DAY

WORLD AND U.S. CONDITIONS were giving us a very perplexing picture. We had the hostage situation in Iran, the Soviet occupancy of Afghanistan, and the major threat to our petroleum supply. Inflation, a never-ending nightmare, could both break us and price us right out of business.

Bob Cook, our circulation manager, and I designed a system for mail distribution of the Cañon City paper, enabling us to begin to pull back from gas-reliant motor routes. I made a resolution that we must follow a similar plan in Longmont and Loveland as well.

I also urged Blaine Hayes to put into place cutbacks for *Daily Record* production personnel. We had to begin to cut personnel because under our operating structure, cuts had to take place in all directions. Newsprint and photo supplies were scheduled for major cost increases, but business was down and the long winter of bad weather had caused further cutbacks in advertising and circulation income.

This was far from a pleasant time in which to do business. We always had known that the true test of a management team was in being capable of surviving the entire cycle of good times, right through a severe recession. We were about to find out if we were a good management team.

Nothing gets one's attention like fighting for survival. Perhaps we were taking up defensive positions a little in advance of major events, but the true picture appeared all too clear—unless we handled the recession, we would lose some newspapers. We were moving in advance of extremes, but there was little doubt of what was happening in these early stages. To many on the outside, our life must have looked very easy and well ordered. Unfortunately, from the inside we knew all too well that the shifting sands of time and the changing economy continually affected us.

The American Newspaper Publishers Association Governmental Affairs Committee met every six months to be updated on events from the nation's capital. We met next on March 11, 1980, and since our last meeting, we had some new problems as well as many of the old ones that were now much worse. The new major concerns were:

1. U.S. economy: Inflation at annual 18 percent, business down, and all costs spiraling upward.
2. Our fellow American citizens, 52 strong, still held hostage by Iranian militants. Negotiations constantly breaking down since their capture 130 days previously.
3. U.S. ambassador being held prisoner by terrorists in Dominican Republic.
4. U.S. defense apparently inadequate and defense budgets need to be increased dramatically. Meanwhile, the U.S. mood is to balance the budget, which generally means a cut in domestic programs.
5. The Soviets are challenging the world by their invasion of Afghanistan. The Cold War appears on the brink of breaking out again. Meanwhile, the Soviets are demanding the U.S. sign the Salt II agreement.
6. As the U.S. and free world industrial powers are threatened by the energy shortage, the OPEC nations keep raising the price of oil. The Soviet moves and Persian Gulf unrest threaten a major disruption of oil supply. This could cause a huge internal disruption.
7. President Carter's popularity has leapt forward, leaving Sen. Ted Kennedy far behind. Meanwhile, Ronald Reagan is in the lead as the GOP standard-bearer, and George Bush is trying hard to catch up. Former President Gerald Ford appears ready to accept the nomination, if he is selected.
8. From six months prior, many major concerns either have worsened materially or been forgotten. No longer did we wonder if the Soviets would challenge Carter—his ineptness was further highlighted with the invasion of Afghanistan and the Soviets' threats surrounding the SALT II agreement.

I covered the Democratic National Convention in August 1980 at Madison Square Garden in New York City.

Before returning home from the ANPA meeting, I stopped in Kankakee, Illinois, and attended the funeral of Len Small. I was deeply saddened, yet happy in a strange euphoria of recollections the service brought to mind. Small was a second-generation newspaperman working alongside his brother and father in the family's six daily operations in Illinois, Indiana, Iowa, and Minnesota. He just recently had been elected chairman and president of ANPA when he was tragically killed in a car accident on March 10.

My life and Ruth's were forever enriched by sharing this quarter of a century with Len Small. He was one of the very best friends I ever had on this earth. In the words of Joe Smith, chairman of the board of ANPA, "We all have gained so much because we have walked together." Both spiritually and physically, Len and I walked so many, many miles together as attorneys and later as community newspaper publishers facing similar challenges. So, it is Goodnight, Sweet Prince. How wonderful "it was that we could spend this time together."

Few challenges are greater than the bar exam, and one of the biggest accomplishments in life is passing it. On May 1, Ruth and I experienced the enormous joy in seeing Dean become a Colorado lawyer. We were so proud and happy for him. We enjoyed the ceremonies at Phipps Auditorium, the reception at the Governor's Mansion, and the luncheon following at the Brown Palace Arms. It may have been raining outside, but we all basked in the warmth of Dean achieving this milestone.

Life continued with its mysterious ways—fatigue, joy, challenge, and ever-changing conditions. The newspapers were slogging along in the wake of the economic downturn. Earnings and advertising volume were down. Interest rates, at a record high of 20 percent, dropped sometimes two points in a single day. Individuals had been severely damaged, and many businesses closed. Those remaining continued to buy advertising, but the larger accounts had cut back drastically. Full-page ads were now a memory.

In earlier years, I had looked forward to an "easy street" based on hard work and success. Now, I realized I dreamed falsely of a mirage. With the passage of time, I came to realize that hard work and ever changing tasks with constant challenges truly was the story of life.

Ruth and I attended the two major national political conventions where we found more exhaustion, disappointment, and despair than joy. We began to realize that one of the most important things before us was to work toward an improved method of selecting presidential candidates. Colorado and most of the West were entirely forgotten at national conventions. The candidates had been selected much earlier, and the final conventions on TV were only rubber stamp extravaganzas. We had much to do to let the public know how this process needed improving, but we rejoiced for now because it appeared America would eventually be saved by the voters.

Ruthann's work in Armstrong's senate campaign in 1978 resulted in a "how to" textbook on public relations. It was a classic, containing many examples of the work she had done for Armstrong. I don't think she realized how significant her landmark publication really was. She was just doing her job, but the pamphlet influenced major events. In 1987 the Colorado Republican Party named her its communication director, a position she held through the 1988 election cycle.

Chapter Thirty-Six

A CENTURY OF NEWSPAPERING IN LOVELAND

THE *LOVELAND DAILY REPORTER-HERALD* commemorated its 100th birthday with a 3-foot-wide by 7-foot-long by 5-inch thick cake that was a replica of a front page. It was shared at an open house with more than 4,000 townspeople who visited the plant to help us celebrate.

In an August 7, 1980, edition paying tribute and sharing the history of Loveland and its newspaper, I wrote:

For the entire staff of the Daily Reporter-Herald, *it is both exciting and challenging to celebrate our 100th birthday.*

A community daily newspaper must serve many people in many different ways. It must mirror the community and faithfully report the ever-changing events of our time. We also must dream and visualize for the future and always have a reverent regard for the past.

We live in the midst of a changing population, and the daily newspaper is the one common link which enables newcomer and native alike to know the community which is their home.

Throughout this century, the men and women of the Daily Reporter-Herald *and its related publications have faced the same challenge in serving their readers. Although the volume of events and news today is much greater, in many ways the production is much easier. Modern printing technology has given us wonderful tools with which to work. Throughout these years, there have been constant changes in upgrading our methods and skills.*

As we look forward to the second century, our staff members visualize an even bigger challenge in telling the day-to-day story of a great community and a most active group of people.

Civic and community events of all kinds were often celebrated with parades. Instead of building floats for every event, we bought a couple of vintage fire trucks for these occasions. One of the veteran pieces of American firefighting memorabilia for many decades with the Minnesota fire departments was a 1929 Model A Ford fire truck. The second fire truck was manufactured as the "Community Fire Fighter," a four-cylinder, five-ton 1923 Stoughton/Peter Pirsch, which served more than four decades in an Iowa fire department. Following these two vehicles' retirement, they were acquired by the Lehman Newspapers and converted to parade vehicles. Suitable for any celebration, they became the newspaper mascots for the *Times-Call*, *Reporter-Herald*, and *Daily Record* at community events and parades. Driving them in parades was one of the great joys of my life, but I had lots of help.

In 1980 Dean began his legal career as an associate of the famed Joe French in the very exciting legal office of French and Stone in Boulder. The variety of their practice provided a splendid opportunity for a young lawyer.

The three dailies and the *Farmer and Miner* were more thought-provoking than ever. Each paper was presenting unique yet substantial hurdles and obstacles because business had been far from good. In fact, for almost a year, it had been poor to lousy. Instead of the breather we needed, the burdens seemed to grow greater.

Bill Johnson, our buoyant sales director, always found the rainbow or silver lining in the dark skies. On October 6, 1980, we had an announcement of the option/purchase of 315 acres in Longmont by Hewlett-Packard. For many years, HP had been a superb mainstay in Loveland, but was likely four years away from building in Longmont. Still this was promising news. (Ultimately, the HP project never happened.)

We were capitalists and therefore great gamblers. As we marched along the endless corridor of newspaper production, we signed contracts for $225,000 in expanding new programs for very advanced advertising equipment and a new front-end production project for the Longmont plant. Foremost in our decision was the expansion of the *Times-Call* equipment to ensure that all three daily papers would be more efficient and standardized.

We also faced $200,000 in business office accounting equipment, which we anxiously awaited with an arrival date scheduled for October 15.

Parade duty often fell to Jim Mitton, facilities, vehicles, and security manager for all of the Lehman newspaper properties, and Bob Cook, circulation manager/vice president, pictured here.

Ruth was the project manager on this badly needed system to get the accounting side of the business more centralized and functioning more effectively.

Ruth was highly criticized by some board members and some upper management for the expense involved, but she made a compelling business argument that it was the right time to get the accounting functions centralized before the business became any larger or more complex. She was most astute in choosing a system designed on solid accounting and business principles but with enough flexibility to allow adaptation and growth over time. I trusted her judgment. This system turned out to be one of our most reliable and solid systems, providing superb service for more than thirty years.

I believed we were on the right track, even though costs were quite unnerving. It was imperative to keep going forward, even though the economy was hurting as it hovered toward a continued downtrend.

High interest rates snuck up on President Carter as they also did in the automotive and real estate sectors. In the fall election, Americans were not too happy with either Carter or Ronald Reagan. However, John Anderson, the independent candidate, was not making the inroads first expected, according to pre-election polls. It was a dull, down period for Americans.

Iraq and Iran had gotten into a major war. The Soviets had been relatively quiet, although foreign policy and military experts had reported America was number two to Russia's military strength. The shortage of fuel was a big threat as fuel costs climbed.

In these very serious times of double-digit inflation, I felt deeply for those poor people on fixed levels of income or savings. While we felt some of the blows, we had vibrant, growing businesses with incomes that could react. Those with fixed or very low incomes could only try to pull in closer and closer.

Gradually I began to feel that the future looked better and that these awful times would pass with a better period ahead. Ronald Reagan certainly offered a great change in leadership. On such occasions, those not in office are elected and those in office are defeated, as people search for a new approach to problems. There always has been an economic theory that business is good in an election year, however, perhaps not since the campaigns of Herbert Hoover or Franklin Roosevelt had an incumbent president run in the midst of such financial and economic adversity.

People were amazed when I recalled the 1976 Democratic Convention in New York and said, "Carter never had been a disappointment to me." He did little or nothing that I did not predict. In fact, I accurately predicted how his term of office would turn out.

We were in the midst of desperate, hard-fought local election campaigns as well, and we were up to our earlobes in hard-fighting, eager candidates. At all levels they were arriving and putting forward their best arguments. Nationally, we had Carter and Reagan. Colorado would reluctantly go for Reagan. These were not everyone's favorite candidates, but they were all we had except for Anderson, who was going downhill fast.

Ruthann had become a major political figure in her own right. Having just closed out her Washington chapter as deputy press secretary for U.S. Senator William Armstrong in his Washington office, she could not resist the challenge of bringing her knowledge into the camp of Mary Estill Buchanan, who was running against Gary Hart for the U.S. Senate seat in 1980. Ruthann became her director of communications and had to leave her cat, Socrates, behind in Washington as the battle bugles called her to the political front.

Indeed we did have a problem and yet many possibilities. We were in a period of very high interest rates. Both state and federal governments were moving with the greatest caution due to taxpayer resistance. Internationally, Iran and the Ayatollah Ruhollah Khomeini's fifty-two U.S. prisoners, continued to occupy the headlines.

Election Day November 4, was at long last over, and Jimmy Carter was defeated. In January 1981 Ronald Reagan became our new president with a Republican Senate majority backing him up. As an American and a human being, I was immensely relieved. Even the sky looked bluer, and with each moment, I felt more alive. The Reagan-Bush ticket very early swept the nation, with Reagan winning forty-four states and Carter successful in only Hawaii, the District of Columbia, Rhode Island, Minnesota, West Virginia, Maryland, and his native Georgia.

It had been a long four years since July 1976 when I watched as Carter was nominated at the Democratic National Convention in New York City. Carter led this nation ever downward.

Our thoughts constantly were centered on Ruthann as she labored desperately on behalf of Mary Estill Buchanan, the Colorado secretary of state and top GOP officeholder, who went down in defeat to incumbent Gary Hart for the U.S. Senate seat. Had Ruthann and other key advisors been aboard even one month earlier, I believe Hart would have been defeated, but such was not the case.

Our Boulder County races were brutal as well. I never remember a more hard-fought local election. Ruth and I were about as tired as if we had been candidates ourselves. Our editorial board, which Ruth and I were members of, interviewed each candidate on their credentials and stands on issues. Each board member wrote editorials, and we produced an election guide with endorsements for all of the offices that were to be filled—local, state and national—which were published just prior to the election. We did this for every election.

Jack Murphy was reelected county commissioner. In the House race, Karen Sekich was narrowly defeated by Candy Dyer, and in the state Senate race, the outstanding Sandy Arnold was defeated by Ron Stewart. In our congressional race, Tim Wirth was reelected in a substantial victory over John McElderry.

Nationally, Democratic kingpins fell right and left. Among the twelve Democratic senators running for reelection, six were defeated: George

McGovern, Frank Church, Warren Maguson, Birch Bayh, Georgia's Herman Talmadge, and Alaska's Clark Gruening. Most were major Senate committee heads. It appeared America was about to make a major change of posture.

Reagan was almost seventy years of age when first elected president, which was remarkable. George Bush, Reagan's vice president, was quite exceptional but not readily recognized by people. He certainly helped Reagan, although he had a very low profile in the campaign.

I fully realized we were blessed as a family to have the unusual introductions and insight as practicing politicians and good newspaper people—at once a rare opportunity and a real test. Ruth and I were the parents of very well-known people in their own right, which was quite a thrill. One of the great joys for us was seeing Dean and Ruthann grow into the fulfillment of living lives of service. Indeed, God blessed each of us individually and as a family.

Ruth and I attended the Denver Club Christmas Ball on December 7. It was 39 years ago I had reported for noon formation at St. John's Military School to hear the announcement that Pearl Harbor had been bombed and that America was at war. This was the 100th anniversary celebration for the Denver Club. On this foggy night, from the 17th floor, Ruth and I looked out on an entirely new Denver that was shooting up in a massive reconstruction of the downtown streets we knew so well. It was most exciting and invigorating to see what was happening to our hometown, the Queen City of the Plains.

The American people were most encouraged by the new administration of Ronald Reagan. We had been going downhill for four years, although the drop had been most apparent in the last fourteen months. Reagan would need about that same amount of time to begin to turn things around.

On December 16, 1980, the prime interest rate went to 21 percent as the nation rushed into an economic dive. Merry Christmas! Perhaps it was a Jimmy Carter finale as he prepared to leave office on January 20. Ronald Reagan and his administration needed to come on strong and fast. As 1980 came to an end, I reflected on the Iranian hostage situation, flat-to-declining business, Carter's inept administration, historic high (21.5 percent) interest rates, OPEC nations repeatedly raising oil prices, the Soviet invasion of Afghanistan and threatening Poland. It was some year, but it certainly could have been worse.

Ruth and I, December 1980

I felt the electronic media faced increasing fractionalization and specialization, and I believed the audiences would become more intense, but would also become much smaller. Meanwhile, the more massive newspaper audience was even more critical because the world was becoming smaller as international events unfolded rapidly. There was a most urgent need to keep the public informed as events occurred. If we thought we were putting out good newspapers today, we had to go the extra steps to be substantially better for tomorrow—not only in content but in timely delivery. Conditions were most pivotal. There would be many tasks and tests ahead for newspapers as they searched for the best way they could serve their communities, municipalities, states, and the nation to meet the demand for accurate and complete coverage.

Locally, a rookie policeman shot and killed two Longmont men of Hispanic heritage; voters rejected public housing; a severe 1979-1980 winter left much damage; two shopping centers competed to locate in Longmont; and a major election returned U.S. Sen. Gary Hart and state

Sen. Ron Stewart to office. County Commissioner Wally Toevs was defeated by Bob Jenkins; and the Pratt Street overpass project began.

We discontinued the *Berthoud Bulletin* because it was very hard to maintain profit margins. Area coverage was continued by absorbing the publication's news and advertising into the Loveland *Reporter-Herald*. Business remained down, with many firms closing entirely.

Everyone around us looked forward to the new administration as Ronald Reagan took over January 20. Within moments of his inauguration, Iran released the fifty-two Americans it had held hostage for 444 days. In a story published in the *Longmont Times-Call*, the Associated Press reported, "As freed American hostages gave new reports Jan. 22 of brutal treatment by their Iranian captors—beatings, mock executions, grim games of Russian roulette, death threats—former President Carter accused Iran of 'savagery against absolutely innocent hostages.'"

On the day after Reagan's inauguration, the Longmont Planning Commission approved the annexation of ninety acres, and plans for a mall in south Longmont began to take shape, which later would be called Twin Peaks Mall. It was scheduled to open in 1983 and be anchored by J. C. Penney, Joslin's, and Sears. Construction was delayed on the 600,000-square-foot shopping center until the following fall, and it finally opened for business August 7, 1985.

We marched on toward uncertain goals. As usual, fatigue accompanied Ruth and me in our steps. What we were doing was important to our communities and our residents. It was not a question of whether our efforts in the past counted. Each dawn brought a new day. We continually had to face new fronts and ever-changing problems. Much was expected of us as well it should have been.

Our accomplishments of the past were history. Our business was as new as tomorrow. Our future rested on our ability to serve and survive in the new frontier of each dawning day. The pace of life quickened. People and events were very mobile. The past was prologue, before us unfolded, day by day, a very dramatic future.

As for the newspapers, the year 1981 began with plans for major production modifications at all three of the daily plants as well as changes and expansion of our management team. Interest rates were again fluctuating upward to 19 percent and were expected to reach 20 percent. Many phases of domestic business had been completely devastated, including automotive, construction, major appliances, and real estate. All of this was reflected in the newspaper industry, but we looked forward to a very busy, innovative year.

Ruthann had made the permanent move from Washington back to Colorado the previous November, this time with her cat. At the time of the move, she changed her name to Lauren to avoid confusion between her and Ruth. Dean joined the firm, succeeding Tom Reeves as editor and general manager of the *Reporter-Herald*. Two new managing editors came on board: Jim Smith in Longmont and Bob Rummel in Loveland.

Lauren returned with some doubts and concerns, which we all had, but I believed she could add a much-needed dimension to our management team while at the same time broaden her own horizons in the front ranks of management. It was a hard challenge to discern the best way to introduce her into the mainstream of the business. She was an outstanding newsperson, which is the foundation and key justification for the entire business. Unless a newspaper management person has an understanding and dedication to news, they are very limited. In many ways we had an excellent staff of executives, but we were passing through a valley that either would lead to lower depths or find us emerging onto a plain of vast expansion.

Onto this front, Lauren entered her newspaper management career at an interesting time in 1981. We were most excited and delighted to have her join us as editorial writer and coordinating news editor of the *Times-Call* and as a member of the board of directors and management committee. Our management team needed to do a far better job. We had trimmed many sails and proved we could be more efficient. I felt this would be a great challenge to each of us to make this association a successful reality, but I believed it would work very well. We certainly were not lacking in demands upon management's time or opportunity.

Although communications was the name of our business, we often had trouble communicating internally between and within departments, management, and staff at the papers. We were not communicating with our subscribers as we should, either. It was an endless contest.

I felt the recent sale of the *Denver Post* to the Times-Mirror Company of Los Angeles was very good because it would revitalize newspaper operations and spirit in all of Colorado. However, I was fully aware it would be only a matter of time before we also would feel the challenge of the Times-Mirror team.

A milestone in technical operations occurred in 1981 when the Associated Press installed satellite dish equipment at the three daily papers in Longmont, Loveland, and Cañon City. Transmissions of national and international news wire articles and photos were received from the Westar II satellite located 23,300 miles out in space. At a speed of 1,200 words per minute, which was phenomenally fast at the time, stories and photos were sent to us from around the world. It forever changed the pace of life in our daily operations.

Ruth was elected president of the Colorado Press Association in 1982 where she worked very hard to write a summary of the First Amendment, remaining most faithful to the law and to the press. In her acceptance speech she noted:

> *We are faced with an economic downturn, and our communications industry as a whole is burgeoning and fractionalizing beyond the wildest dreams of even science-fictions writers.*
>
> *As we tighten our belts and learn to sell our products against new and different competition, we continue to face the eternal problem of protecting our right to publish news without government interference. We continue to have the challenge of not only protecting the people's right to know but, increasingly, needing to make people want to know so they can and will participate in our government process.*

One Friday evening at the Longmont plant, I narrowly escaped being shot when a sizable bullet came through my office window as the *Times-Call* newsroom staff was wrapping up stories for the Saturday morning paper. Because there were windows between my office and the newsroom, the staff was sent flying for cover. The bullet was fired from the alley north of Fourth Avenue between Coffman and Terry Streets. Unlike in *Casablanca*, there was some difficulty in rounding up the usual suspects. Although we never had complete proof of who the culprit was, we had a fairly good idea. But the real problem was there were several distinct possibilities.

Longmont police detectives interviewed some individuals of interest, but nothing ever came of these. We had a rather sleepy police department at the time and a full accounting or explanation as to the reason for this cowardly deed was never given. Of course, no one stepped up and took credit for it, either.

The *Times-Call* became a seven-days-a-week operation with the introduction of a Sunday edition on July 7, 1985. I wrote a letter to our readers explaining the milestone we had just crossed:

Dear Reader,
In your hands you hold the first Sunday edition published in the 115-year history of the Daily Times-Call.
We have considered it for years and planned it for months. A Sunday newspaper with all of its features is far different from the daily editions published six other days of the week.
Throughout America, only a handful of daily newspapers each year make the major step to introduce a Sunday edition. This is not only a milestone for the newspaper, but a forward step for the people of Boulder County and the entire Greater St. Vrain Valley.
The new seven-days-a-week operation has changed the roles and lives of hundreds of people who work together to bring you this newspaper. Many of its sections require planning and development weeks in advance for each Sunday edition.
Late-breaking news often is being gathered, edited and processed only minutes before the presses roll during the early hours of Sunday morning.
The Sunday edition has been designed to bring each member of the family memorable and enjoyable experiences in weekend reading. Each week, a new edition of "Prime Time" will give you a handy mini-magazine with the area's most complete listings of TV and cable schedules.
The Sunday Times-Call Magazine *will showcase a wide variety of news articles and background pieces by staff writers, outside contributors and Associated Press correspondents. And, of course, there are many other features, including the color comics section. But you will discover these for yourself.*
Local, regional and national advertisers not only make this edition possible, but they also are bringing the latest in fashions, bargains and marketing developments. Hundreds of individual advertisers join in the lively classified section with their own messages.

First and foremost, we are a newspaper for our community. But our pages also must mirror the state, nation and world in which we live.

On behalf of the entire newspaper staff, we thank all of you for making this challenge and opportunity a reality. We look f orward to serving you and enriching your life with information and enjoyable reading.

 Faithfully yours,
Ed Lehman
Editor and Publisher

In 1985 we created a new department called Information Systems. Its main purpose was to implement technology changes to standardize production procedures. We hoped this would give us more efficiency and help us contain costs corporate-wide. Ruth and I felt this department, placed at the corporate level, would enable us to have better control in directing each division toward our overall goals. Eventually we would be successful in realizing these objectives.

The national unemployment rate dropped from 10 percent in 1982 to a five-year low of 7 percent in August 1985. U.S. inflation plummeted from a high of 16 percent to around 3.7 percent. Reaganomics was beginning to have an effect on Longmont, Loveland, and Cañon City, which were struggling to strengthen their economies.

We had an exceptional year in 1985 with awards for all of the papers. The highlight was the *Cañon City Daily Record*, whose advertising staff was honored as number one in a nine-state region for advertising excellence by the Rocky Mountain Ad Managers. The paper also came in first among Colorado daily papers for overall advertising excellence, and the news staff received an award for its community service.

In November 1985, Ruth and I traveled to China on a tour sponsored by the Chinese Ministry of Justice. We spent three weeks visiting Beijing (commonly known as Peking), Nanjing, and Wuhan, located midway between Beijing and Canton (Guangzhou). The tour included briefings on subjects covering a wide range of topics in this very active nation.

This was one of the reports I wrote about the trip for the *Times-Call:*

Officials in Nanjing, a classic, tree-lined former capital expressed pride that in their province they had 604 of China's 20,000 lawyers. One-hundred-eleven of their lawyers were women and their number was growing in China's legal and court circles at that time.

Since the end of the decade-long Cultural Revolution, China's legal system had been rapidly emerging. In Beijing, there was the Institute of Law with 150 specialists studying statutes and decisions around the world. Their spokesmen expressed an interest in all law, but admitted their greatest interest was in economic law.

The Ministry of Justice also had a division of legal studies. It exercised close control over five independent law schools and legal departments or schools in thirty Chinese universities.

Obtaining the services of a lawyer in China was much different from the United States. A lawyer in China handled your case with loyalty to the law as their yardstick and treatment of the facts with absolute frankness. Loyalty to the law and not the client was, and still is, paramount. A few lawyers talked with our group and indicated they were planning to set up private practices—a much needed field by international businesses seeking operations in China in those days.

The individual is protected and has rights under the Chinese Constitution and fundamental laws. When we visited there had recently been enacted a new fundamental criminal and civil procedure system of laws on a trial basis.

These basic legal landmarks had been enacted by the National People's Congress meeting in Beijing. In turn, within the twenty-two provinces, three municipalities, and five autonomous regions, there also were people's congresses. These groups dared not enact or contradict any laws enacted by the National People's Congress. However, at their various levels, these Congresses did select the judges for the four levels of courts. These judges served as presidents or vice-presidents without the assistance of juries. They also conducted their own investigations and stressed mediation in 10 out of every 11 cases before them. They reported mediation was successful in 85 percent of their cases.

> *The levels of court included the Supreme People's Court of the Republic of China. Next, in the provinces, municipalities and autonomous regions were the Higher People's Courts. Below them were the Intermediate People's Court and under them, the People's Courts in counties, rural areas, districts and municipalities. Appeal was always available to the next court level and it was mandatory in cases of the death penalty. We also explored criminal law more fully and visited reformatories, work-study institutions, and penitentiaries....*
>
> *Among their deepest desires were to anchor their system of government and individual rights so as to prevent a Cultural Revolution ever again being unleashed....*
>
> *Because of China's more than fifty dialects, many legal proceedings were held in the native dialect. The Ministry of Justice also was charged with the education of all the Chinese regarding the changing law and the basic law. This was an ongoing responsibility, along with overseeing the training of all lawyers.*
>
> *Lawyers, regardless of their standing in their own nations, were limited in their scope of action in China. Some arrived only to find they really were outsiders. In 1985 various Chinese governmental agencies sought to offer the best of legal representation and advice to international business people. Close observers told us that the Chinese sought simple contracts, but managed to center in on pivotal facts. Others complained that a negotiation constantly shifted ground and parties. Regardless of the opinions, many outsiders did conduct successful business in China.*
>
> *One of the most unusual facets of China's legal world was that judges were not lawyers. Instead of being learned in the law, they were selected for their knowledge of the law, good morality, and basic fairness. Courts did not follow the precedent decided in earlier cases. They applied general theories, which were constantly emerging.*

In 1986 I was greatly honored to become a trustee of the Boettcher Foundation, serving in this capacity from 1986 to 2000.

By August 1986 the *Times-Call* reported the U.S. gross national product showed the national economy expanding at its fastest rate in five years. In Cañon City, the *Daily Record* contributed its fair share to help the economy with the purchase of the *Sun-Trader,* a weekly shopper, from Guy and Marcia Wood.

To speed up production turnaround time and computerize plate processing at the *Daily Record*, a 3M camera and Deadliner equipment were purchased. Also, major remodeling was done to the binder/mailroom and pressroom to accommodate two additional Goss Community press units, bringing capacity on the press to 24 broadsheet and 48 tab pages. By the end of the year, remodeling was completed to both floors of the *Daily Record* and a fully integrated editorial, classified, and display advertising computer system went into full operation.

In September 1986 President Reagan was asking for assistance: "If Congress will help me to control domestic spending, to work for freer and fairer trade and to reduce tax rates by passing our fair share tax plan for all Americans, then we can reach our goal. We can unleash a decade of growth and create 10 million new jobs in the next four years."

Longmont businesspeople signaled their desire to participate in the economic recovery when they elected local Realtor Ken Pratt as president of the Economic Development Association of Longmont in 1986.

While the economy improved, the Reagan administration ran into other problems. On July 7, 1987, Marine Col. Oliver North conceded he had made the "grossest misjudgment of my life" in his involvement in the diversion of funds from Iranian weapons sales to the Nicaraguan Contras, but he denied taking any of the funds. Senate Iran-Contra hearings ended in August with Republicans joining Democrats in denouncing the secrecy and deception that allowed the affair to flourish. Republican Sen. Warren Rudman of New Hampshire condemned North and National Security Advisor John M. Poindexter for shredding documents, lying to Congress and the attorney general, and withholding information from President Reagan.

In keeping with the nation's economic recovery in 1987, the newspapers experienced tremendous growth. The *Cañon City Daily Record* was brought in as a third division—the Royal Gorge Publishing Company—joining the Times-Call Publishing Company and the Loveland Publishing Company under the umbrella of the newly-created Lehman Communications Corporation. I remained publisher and chairman of the board and took on the responsibilities of chief executive officer for the corporation. Dean was named its president and chief operating officer.

As our nation's leadership changed again in 1988, this time with Vice President George H. W. Bush being elected president, so too our management team continued to evolve. At the *Reporter-Herald*, Bob Rummel was named editor and general manager, and Ken Amundson moved into the managing editor position.

We published an annual special section at each of our newspapers reviewing the people, places, and events in the communities we served. We also looked ahead to the opportunities and tasks facing each of these communities in the coming twelve months. In March 1988, I wrote in the *Longmont Daily Times-Call*:

> *We again welcome our readers to many enjoyable and informative glimpses of life in Colorado's Greater St. Vrain Valley. Here you will find the stories about our many communities and their people who make them a living reality.*
>
> *As we review the edition, we realize there has never before been a time when we have had more "dynamic horizons", but we need to have both the vision and spirit to reach them. Certainly we have much to be thankful for in our area in the heart of the very glorious State of Colorado. And yet, there is so much to do and accomplish because our world has changed. New dreams must be crafted and new goals established.*
>
> *Colorado's vigorous Gov. Roy Romer is challenging the people of this state to go forth and attain new economic achievements. In his first 14 months in office, he has led an international campaign to get Colorado into the forefront of development. Earlier this week in Longmont, Governor Romer particularly praised the people of the City of Longmont for their role in international development, particularly toward the surging and emerging Pacific Rim nations.*
>
> *Our home in Boulder County is one of America's great centers for technological development and manufacturing. In more recent years, we have faced massive layoffs. Fortunately, that downtrend now is reversed. In January, it officially was reported the county's unemployment level dropped to 5.1 percent. Welcome news, indeed.*
>
> *More good news: Longmont's lagging sales and use tax revenues for February, 1988 exceeded a similar period a year ago by 14.1 percent.*

During the past five years researchers at the University of Kentucky conducted a penetrating review of environmental and economic factors in 253 urban counties throughout the United States. Recently, the Kentucky officials announced Pueblo County, Colorado placed in the No. 1 spot and our own Boulder County placed 12th or in the top five percent.

Today, the leaders of the dozen communities in the Greater St. Vrain Valley all are viewing the horizon to design a better future for their citizens of today and tomorrow. As we look toward positive steps, certainly our first choice must be for a more robust economy. Meanwhile there is not an economic or organizational endeavor that is not experiencing the necessity of conducting business in ever different ways from past years.

We all are realizing that as we live for today we must be planning and investing for the future. As the pioneers who went before us, we must turn to thinking in larger plans and not cripple our future by petty thoughts. In the Northern Colorado area around us, many cities boldly have eyed the future and have doubled and tripled their city limits. This paves the way for coordinated, long range planning and efficient development.

Of international interest on the horizon is the development less than an hour away of one of the world's great airports. The location of this multi-billion dollar project is geographically unique. Here will be an international crossroads covering all points of the compass and efficiently serving the continents of the world.

Together our future is what we make it. Before us truly are dynamic horizons, many greater than our civilization has faced before.

In these exciting times we rededicate our staff and ourselves to our newspaper motto:

"To Build a Better World, Start in Your Own Community."

In 1984 we had built a 14,100-square-foot warehouse annex beside a railroad spur to receive and house the rolls of newsprint. By 1987 this would serve as a temporary home for the circulation department during major construction of a 22,500-square-foot addition to the main Longmont plant, which more than doubled the plant's size. Completed in

The Longmont Daily Times-Call *in 1988, after construction of a major addition and complete remodeling to the existing building that more than doubled its size.* (Pellegren Architectural Company rendering)

the fall of 1988, it allowed the newspaper to remain in the downtown area. This marked a big change for circulation as their operations became more computerized and fully integrated with the business office, with a vast network of motor routes established.

The decade ended with the destruction of the Berlin Wall and the "disintegration of communism in Eastern Europe. Mikhail S. Gorbachev's efforts to lead the Soviet Union into a freer society" was reported in the *Times-Call* as the most significant story of 1989 and perhaps the decade. Eastern European countries such as Bulgaria, Czechoslovakia, East Germany, and Hungary witnessed thousands of angry people in the streets demanding eviction of the old Communist guard and a voice in government, with a more accessible and unrestricted social order. Solidarity, a trade union, won an election in Poland and began to build ties with the West to try to pull their country out of severe poverty. But Communism did not simply vanish, not by a longshot. It merely went underground.

Chapter Thirty-Seven

1990s—WARS WITHOUT AND WITHIN

THE *CAÑON CITY DAILY RECORD* won national awards when the Inland Press Association awarded it first place in investigative reporting and in editorial writing. In addition to recognition from the Colorado Press Association and the Inland Press Association, the *Longmont Daily Times-Call* and the *Loveland Daily Reporter-Herald* received top awards from the National Newspaper Association. We always celebrated these successes because we viewed them as a true measure of our exactitude.

The *Daily Record* inaugurated a non-duplicating Total Market Coverage (TMC) product named *Marketplace*, which was distributed throughout Fremont and Custer Counties, and a stand-alone computer system was installed to run financial worksheets and word processing. Don Heath was named corporate assistant/general manager, and Daryl Beall was named editor and general manager of the *Daily Record*.

The *Times-Call* and *Reporter-Herald* were two of the first newspapers in the United States to convert in 1992 to total pagination—a process that enabled editors to electronically design and layout pages, integrating placement of news articles, photos, graphics, and advertising, all within a group of linked software applications.

This changeover was a massive undertaking with many moving parts and would take almost two years to complete. Newspapers, unlike most other industries, produce an entirely new product each day. Between the *Times-Call*, *Reporter-Herald*, and *Daily Record*, we were producing a tremendous number of pages each day, along with special sections and commercial print jobs.

Nationally, after one term, another contentious presidential election in 1992 saw Arkansas Gov. Bill Clinton defeat President George H. W. Bush and Texas billionaire Ross Perot in a three-way race to become the nation's 42nd president. In 1993 the U.S. began its bombing campaign in Kosovo and sent in troops. Yasser Arafat and Yitzhak Rabin shook hands on the White House lawn, ending the taboo on formal recognition between Israel and Palestine. Although the two men signed a declaration of principle on limited Palestinian self-rule as the first step toward overall peace between the two longtime enemies, peace has remained as elusive as ever.

The year 1993 was exceptional in its violence at home and in the nation's sense of insecurity with the World Trade Center bombing that killed six and injured 1,000. Two years later, on April 19, 1995, 168 people died in the bombing of the Alfred P. Murrah building in Oklahoma City. Timothy McVeigh and Terry Nichols were charged and convicted of the bombing. Their separate trials were moved to Denver where the courthouse became fortress-like.

Everyone, from custodians to the U.S. attorney, had to pass through metal detectors that checked for anything that might be used as a weapon. It wouldn't be the last time violence invaded our public spaces in the 1990s, leading to a national debate on how to strike a balance between public access and safety.

The late 1990s did bring to a close nearly twenty years of death and destruction by "Unabomber" Ted Kaczynski. Arrested in a tiny, remote cabin in Montana, Kaczynski was responsible for placing or mailing bombs that killed three people and injured 23. A Harvard-trained mathematician, he pled guilty to the mail bombings allegedly as part of his campaign against technological tyranny and was sentenced to life in prison. He is being held in the maximum security section of the federal penitentiary near Cañon City.

Naturally, newspapers and the electronic media reported on these events as they unfolded. The nation and world were aghast at the sheer inhumaneness of stories surrounding the people and events of this decade. Criticism aimed at the extraordinary media attention given to violent events posed the supposition that, in fact, the extensive coverage was why they proliferated. While it is not healthy or productive to dwell on these types of events and repeatedly report when there is nothing new to reveal, likewise it is the right of every citizen to know what is happening in their local communities, their states, their country, and the world.

In celebration of the Times-Call's *125th anniversary I drove the company's ceremonial 1923 Stoughton fire truck while Bob Cook, former vice president of circulation, navigated the parade route for me.*

In 1994, we purchased a building in Loveland owned in part by Richard Ball at 205 East Fifth Avenue in preparation for moving the *Loveland Daily Reporter-Herald* operations across the street to the newly remodeled site. We began laying the groundwork for more computerization in the ensuing years by converting each of the three daily papers' library archives into electronic format, and introduced computers and scanners to standardize and streamline graphics for news and advertising.

A short two years later in 1996 we built a new building for the *Cañon City Daily Record* and added two units to the Goss Community press. Updated front-end advertising and news computer systems were installed as well.

In an April 21, 1996, commemorative edition of the *Times-Call*, the paper shared its rich history, as well as how the town of Longmont had grown and embraced its newspaper over the years:

> *As the community daily newspaper, we gather and present history in a hurry. Each daily edition is a new time capsule highlighting the epic march through time of mankind and the people of the Greater St. Vrain Valley. Often our pages are the first to welcome in print a new birth and the last to express a written word of farewell to a life.*
>
> *We serve as a community bulletin board and our editorial pages give people the chance to express opinions and consider new thoughts. From the earliest time when a small seedling of civilization began here, our pages have served as the chronicle for a vigorous people calling Longmont and a dozen surrounding communities their home.*
>
> *We have cheered the successes and have been deeply saddened by failures and tragedy. With each passing year, we endeavor to lead our communities toward an ever better tomorrow. The greatest stories of the future are yet to be written.*
>
> —Ed Lehman, Times-Call Publishing Company

A sad ending to 1996 was the death of JonBenet Ramsey, a little girl found dead in her parents' home in Boulder on December 26. We learned much later that the grand jury voted to indict the parents, but the district attorney decided not to proceed. As I write this, some twenty years later, it remains one of Colorado's more infamous unsolved murders. This was a most unusual case with numerous rumors gaining momentum each day. Some media outlets declared the father of the little girl to be guilty, when actually there was never enough evidence to substantiate that claim. Dean superbly held the reins, insisting only the facts be reported and not to jump to any conclusions. I soon began to feel we would likely never know what had happened that terrible night.

In 1997, the Colorado General Assembly recognized Ruth for her "prestigious awards in the field of journalism and her invaluable contributions to the Colorado community." Rep. Vi June of Westminster spoke about Ruth, "It has been my privilege to know Ruth for a number of years during my years of newspaper publishing. At one point I served on the

Colorado Press Association with Ruth and I have to confess to you folks, she is tough, tougher than I am. But she always tempered her toughness with fairness and she was a real asset to the newspaper business and the newspaper association." Colorado Press Women named Ruth Communicator of Achievement, and the Colorado Area Council of the American Business Women's Association recognized her as a Woman of Distinction.

In February 1997 the *Times-Call* and *Reporter-Herald* launched their first Web sites. At first, we were slow to embrace this technology because we viewed it as competition to our print products. Over time we came to see print and the Internet as complementary to each other, expanding our readership to different segments of subscribers.

On June 1 of the same year, the *Reporter-Herald* began its Sunday edition, making it a seven-days-a-week paper. Assistant Managing Editor Troy Turner was named managing editor of the *Reporter-Herald*, and Ken Amundson moved into a newly created position as assistant to the publisher.

In what would become our last newspaper purchase, we bought the *Louisville Times*, *Lafayette News*, and *Erie Review*, a group of weeklies headquartered in Lafayette, from Percy and Carolyn Conarroe, long-time Colorado newspaper owners and fellow members of the Colorado Press Association. We would eventually expand this group to encompass another weekly in the town of Superior.

Later, in cost-saving moves we would merge all of the weeklies, combining the news and advertising content of each community, into one publication called *Colorado Hometown Weekly,* eventually centralizing all offices at the building in Lafayette. Ultimately, all personnel and production would be consolidated at the main plant in Longmont.

The Denver Broncos won the first of back-to-back Super Bowls in 1997, beating the Green Bay Packers 31 to 24 in Super Bowl XXXII; the following year they would beat the Atlanta Falcons in Super Bowl XXXIII 34 to 19. Nationally, the year ended with the House Judiciary Committee debating whether to impeach President Clinton for lying to a grand jury.

Big changes took place throughout the *Times-Call* and *Reporter-Herald* in 1998 when both dailies converted to morning delivery. This affected all aspects of business—from advertising, newsgathering, and

In 1998 Ruth and I were inducted into the Boulder County Business Hall of Fame. Ruth was so happy that day. She was really proud of the recognition.

circulation to production and distribution—making us truly a 24/7/365 operation. Deadlines for every department had to be adjusted and round-the-clock staffing allowed for, especially in the production and press departments. At this time Rick Carpenter became managing editor of the *Loveland Daily Reporter-Herald*.

In April 1999 two students killed twelve classmates and one teacher at Columbine High School in Littleton before turning their hatred and their guns on themselves. Dozens of students stayed home in the days and weeks that followed amid rumors something similar would happen in Longmont. Although school officials investigated each rumor, all proved to be false.

It gave the nation pause. The combined death toll stood at 186 between the World Trade Center, Oklahoma City, and Columbine. Suddenly workplaces, schools, and even our places of worship no longer felt safe. Americans killing Americans in numbers and ferocity not seen since the Civil War was terrifying the country.

That same year what had begun as an investigation several years earlier of a land deal called Whitewater led to a national scandal. Another scandal would lead to only the second impeachment and eventual acquittal of a sitting American president. Andrew Johnson, the 17th U.S. president and successor to Abraham Lincoln after his assassination, was impeached in 1868 but survived. The country was at once repelled and riveted by the president's dalliances, but after thirteen months, Longmont residents heaved a collective sigh of relief as the president was acquitted on charges of perjury and obstruction of justice. Although national polls showed most Americans believed the Senate was right to acquit Clinton, both Colorado senators, Ben Nighthorse Campbell and Wayne Allard, voted to convict him.

Rumblings surrounding computer systems being unable to handle the move into the twenty-first century had begun surfacing, making headlines worldwide. Known by the acronym Y2K, the problem generally focused on differences between the Julian and Gregorian calendars. The newspaper industry was no exception to growing concern over vulnerability for its computer systems. Lehman Communications embarked on a series of studies to determine what could be salvaged from its existing systems. It soon was discovered that some systems required major upgrades to software and hardware, while others had to be replaced entirely.

Although our goal had never been to be on the "bleeding edge" of technology, we often found ourselves on the "leading edge," which in this case meant anticipating and acting well ahead of the curve to replace and update the tools of our trade. This two-year project to fix what we could and replace what was unfixable for Y2K got us out of the danger zone well before the clock struck midnight on December 31, 1999. No champagne corks were popped, but relief reverberated throughout the newspapers as we avoided catastrophe and turned Y2K into a non-event.

Ruth G. Lehman, was honored by the Colorado General Assembly for her many civic contributions to Colorado. She had been associate editor of the Times-Call, *editorial page editor, and business manager during her forty-year newspaper career, which also included presiding over the Colorado Press Association and serving as board member and treasurer of the Inland Press Association. She also belonged to the American Society of Newspaper Editors, the Society of Professional Journalists and the Institute of Newspaper Controllers and Finance Officers.*

Chapter Thirty-Eight

A TERRIBLE LOSS

SIMULTANEOUSLY AS WE WERE APPROACHING A NEW DECADE and a new century, I was 74 and in the midst of experiencing one of the absolute worst times of my life. Ruth, my wife of 50 years, was deeply ill with amyloidosis, a debilitating and mysterious blood plasma cell disorder that had made her an invalid.

All our hopes and chips rested with the Mayo Clinic in Rochester, Minnesota, where she was being treated. In September 1999 we returned for another four-week treatment of TDox, a heavy chemical designed to close down on the blood platelets that crowded her lungs. Meanwhile, she was on forced oxygen 24 hours a day, but this was certainly not a cure. It only treated the symptoms and deepened the medical mystery.

By mid-October it was apparent the TDox had failed. We tried to find other cures. We had heard fighting this disease could be slow, but I wondered if there was any progress at all. I told Ruth that I thought I had aged much more in 1999 than in any previous year. In retrospect I realized our last four vacations were disappointing, and I became convinced that amyloidosis had been creeping in for a long, long time.

On April 9, 2000, Ruth succumbed to the disease. She fought a valiant fight and struggled for so long, in fact much longer than the two years she was given when she was first diagnosed. Unfortunately for Ruth, at the time of her illness, research funding for the disease was almost nonexistent. In 2016 the form of the disease she had, AL Amyloidosis, strikes more than 4,500 people each year in the U.S. While funding for research has increased, it is still a deadly disease. Although there have been successful remissions involving bone marrow transplants, this is not the solution for everyone.

Ruth and I shared our lives in all we did for almost fifty-one years. We were truly blessed with a wonderful life together and our two children, who were drawing close to the prime of their lives. Our two grandchildren were independent young adults, following their individual dreams and life pursuits.

I forever rejoice that Ruth and I had a nearly perfect marriage. It was a blessing and each day an enriching experience. Marriage is a mystery and a fearful gamble by two players. But if they win, it is the greatest and most important of all experiences in life. It is not that there will not be storms and heavy seas, but the deep fabric can be a strength that deeply enriches a man and a woman as they clasp hands together and stand against the world. Since problems and challenges can be so numerous, like a great building they must start on a great foundation. I would not realize the full extent of this loss until much later.

PART FIVE
Entering the 21st Century

Chapter Thirty-Nine

FIRST DECADE— 2000–2010

AMAZINGLY AND FORTUNATELY, the business continued upward. Progress was most encouraging and the newspapers were a godsend as I faced a new phase in my life, without Ruth. I felt that ahead were better times, although amid greater challenges. Longmont's population was now 71,093. Lauren, vice president of Lehman Communications, stepped in to fill the role of chief financial officer. We heard that our great friend and former *Reporter-Herald* general manager Tom Reeves and his wife, Bev, had returned to Loveland from New Mexico. We contacted Tom, and he agreed to return and serve on our corporate board of directors.

As we embarked on 2001, I wrote a column that appeared in each newspaper's newsletter, and laid out what I saw as our tasks and opportunities for the year ahead:

> *As the New Year rapidly comes upon us, let us look down the pathway of time into the near future. There will be a new administration and one rule is foremost in each of our lives: change will continue everywhere.*
>
> *The longevity secret of daily newspapers is that we also are constantly changing. We are forever challenged to make the newspaper edition more interesting to better serve our many audiences. We are looking ahead to new features, more exciting artwork and the development of new major stories.*
>
> *Certainly the near future brings the challenge of overhauling our entire election machinery. All of us would like to look far sharper than our sister Florida citizens and officials. Yet on a statewide and local basis, how do we measure up? Are we*

consistent throughout our voting districts? How efficient are our voting machines? Are our election laws out of date?

Hopefully, all balloting for federal offices will be sound and consistent. This also will bring many local methods up to higher efficiency. Only newspapers and the printed word are most capable of bringing order out of unfathomable chaos.

The campaign of Al Gore and many other candidates suddenly tore the mask from voting practices and procedures throughout the nation.

As the eye and ear trusted to serve the public, we must develop our own techniques of rapidly and efficiently covering public meetings.

We are doing field experiments with rapid transmitting equipment. Along the same lines, we are scheduling field experiments with electronic portable computers, which will give our advertising staffers great research tools at their fingertips.

We believe 2001 will be a new year of combined sharing of stories and ideas between our various teams of associates. Together we have much strength, but it takes planning and cross-training to bring these ideas into reality.

The year 2001 will be exceptional for our devotion to new surveys to help us gain in-depth analysis. We also want to share the ideas and observations from our associates in every area of our companies.

How can we do our jobs better? How can we serve more of our fellow citizens with the information so vital to their success?

We need your help. In turn, be assured of the dedication and desire of the company leadership. Together, we must work together as a team and pledge to each other that this can be one of the best years of our careers.

Although I continued to find great satisfaction in my work I was a bit at loose ends and quite lonely following Ruth's death. It took me a while to adjust to the loss. Longtime *Times-Call* employee and Longmont resident Connie Coffield came to my rescue, and our friendship blossomed.

Connie came to the Longmont area with her family from Rapid City, South Dakota. Her father, Richard Klein, built several theaters in Longmont, and Connie managed them for him. Shortly after he sold the theaters, she came to work at the *Times-Call* as manager of the Newspaper in Education program, working closely with the local school district to use our newspaper as an educational tool in the classrooms. She was also responsible for promoting the newspaper in numerous community events, eventually managing the promotions department. On behalf of the newspaper, Connie worked to coordinate many events of importance to the Longmont community, including the Hunger Hurts Community Food Drive, Winter Warmth Coat Drive, Duck Race, and the Sunrise Stampede. She was with the paper for more than twenty-five years.

In January 2001 Connie and I were married. In the fifteen years we've been together, she has taken wonderful care of me. Being a single child, I didn't know what I was in for when I married a woman who was from a large family! She has shown me that large family gatherings are great fun. She is a wonderful hostess and often entertains our family and friends. I enjoy her hobby of gardening almost as much as she does, especially the fruits and vegetables she grows and preserves. Over the years we have taken some great trips, some of which have turned into exciting adventures in themselves, but those details will have to be covered in another book.

Fall was always a busy time at the papers with the resumption of many activities after summer break. From city and county endeavors to state legislative and national congressional government sessions reconvening, all departments at the newspapers were humming with new undertakings. However, on one particular bright fall day full of hope in September 2001, America was shaken to its core as it witnessed what has come to be known as the 9/11 attacks. Terrorists, commandeering several commercial jetliners, crashed them into the Twin Towers of the World Trade Center in New York City, and the Pentagon building. A struggle with passengers on the third plane ended tragically with it plunging into a Pennsylvania farm field. Of course, everyone on board all of the planes was killed, in addition to so many citizens in the buildings and surrounding areas, including many first responder firemen. Just about every kind of movement and pursuit of commerce came to a screeching halt as the government assessed these separate but connected incidents of terror. America and the world were in shock.

We covered 9/11 just as we would any national emergency as the facts began to unfold in the cities and states where the jets had crashed. In addition, each of our newspapers tried to bring a personal scale to the enormity

In 2003 Connie and I hosted an "old-timer's" dinner, where everyone took time from reminiscing for a group photo. From left: Blaine Hayes, retired production manager and vice president; Jean Cook (Bob Cook's wife); Dale Carr, production manager and vice president; Bev Reeves (Tom Reeves' wife); Tom Reeves, Lehman Communications board member; myself; Alyce Hayes, retired advertising composition supervisor and Blaine's wife; Bob Cook, retired circulation manager and vice president; Carol Carr (Dale's wife); and Leatha Flanders, retired society editor.

of each incident from a local perspective, interviewing people with family or friends lost or touched in any way.

The events of 9/11 have been reviewed countless times in still photos and video and written news accounts. The immediate facts and passions as recorded by journalists at the time now have been augmented by a long-view perspective. Both are history. Like a rock dropped into a lake, I felt the ripple effects would be felt for years, even decades to come. In 2016 repercussions still reverberate.

By 2002 Longmont had completed construction of a new recreation center, a museum and cultural center, and improvements were made to Roosevelt Park including the senior center.

Internally major steps were taken in replacing the outside network consultants and a change in the leadership of the information technology department. Almost immediately, under the leadership of Suzanne Barrett, long-time employee and member of the technology department since its inception in 1985, significant improvements began to take shape to the basic design of the corporation's computer network and telecommunications foundation. Equipment was upgraded at each division, tying production and telecommunications together, resulting in vastly improved performance and improved security. With these changes and major upgrades to the editorial and archive systems, we achieved cross-media capabilities. We long had a plan, since back at the beginning of the computerization process in the 1980s, to choose a path giving us flexibility for change and growth in connection and communication between all systems at all newspaper sites. At last we were seeing these plans become reality.

However, just as we were making great progress in so many important areas, our dear friend and trusted colleague Tom Reeves suffered a fall and died in March 2003. He was a crucial counselor and wise prognosticator into the future of the newspaper industry, so vital to our studies and decisions for upcoming projects affecting all operations.

In 2004 we embarked upon a three-year transformation project for the business office that gave managers at each division the ability to approve invoices electronically and provided direct deposit of employee paychecks. The human resources department was more fully integrated into the business office structure with provisions for electronic timesheets and employee self-service programs, giving employees access to their vacation and work schedules and other benefits programs.

Each of these carefully calculated steps were part of a larger plan to expedite and streamline accounting processes while enhancing time management and cost controls. However, they were never intended to completely replace the human element of checks and balances. We viewed our computer systems as important tools, but believed heartily in the verification of all information by humans at key points of data entry and exit.

During periods of growth and prosperity, the corporation invested heavily in the business and in our people, as we valued both equally in the success of our newspapers. We always believed ahead was a greater tomorrow.

At headquarters in Longmont in 2006, in the heart of production operations, film image setters in the camera/plate department were replaced with modern equipment and a page workflow system—both key components for centralizing and managing the production flow from each division for commercial and news operations. Bringing together all elements of the pages from the advertising, editorial, and graphics systems and sending the completed images directly to the plates where they were subsequently fitted on the press for printing eliminated a number of steps in the production process. Once again this placed us on the cutting edge of newspaper technology.

These projects to modernize production and delivery of the newspapers required buy-in from staff and customers alike. Advertisers and commercial customers were most appreciative of our efforts to accommodate their individual needs and offer ever more timely service. However, often it seemed the strongest opposition and push back came from our own employees. In the end we eventually achieved our goals, but this internal resistance to change made remaining focused on producing the newspapers and accommodating our commercial customers' needs more difficult and certainly added stress to each day.

Longmont was named an All-America City in 2006 and one of the "Best Places to Live" by CNN/*Money Magazine*. At an elevation of 4,979 feet above sea level and with more than 1,500 acres of parks and open space, the city is perfect for outdoor enthusiasts and has become home to several high-tech companies.

In 2007, management changes were taking place at the *Reporter-Herald*. With the retirement of Bob Rummel, general manager and editor, Ken Amundson moved into that position. Christine Kapperman was promoted to managing editor. Rummel would continue to serve a crucial role as a member of the board of directors for several more years.

After nearly a decade of discussion, planning meetings with various architects, attending industry trade shows, and traveling to newspapers throughout the country, the decision was finally made to purchase a new press. There was an enormous amount of planning and synchronization to bring this about in a timely manner.

The year 2008 was a significant year, both positively and negatively. A major development at the newspapers was Lauren's decision to sell her shares in the business and leave her positions as chief financial officer and senior vice president of Lehman Communications Corporation. Dean and I took over sole ownership.

On March 14, groundbreaking took place for a new joint printing center, named Lehman Communications Print Facility. It would be built on property we already owned east of the Burlington Northern Santa Fe (BNSF) railroad line that runs through Berthoud, a small agricultural community midway between Longmont and Loveland.

Groundbreaking on March 14 for the new 62,000-square-foot newspaper printing center that opened for business in May 2009. It was a grand day.

With a project of this size, once equipment is chosen, financial analysis and studies completed, architectural drawings rendered, and ground broken, the die is cast. We had set into motion something greater than the sum of its parts, and it would not be easy to change course or stop the forward momentum.

A new German-made *manroland Uniset 75* press was delivered by ship to Houston, Texas, where it was loaded onto five semis and driven overland to the Berthoud site. It was a real joy to me to watch this take shape. Like a giant ship, the press rose up piece by intricate piece to become reality. The project had been fraught with so many delays and differences of opinion that it truly was a miracle it ever got off the drawing board and actually completed.

Lehman Communications Print Facility, located in Berthoud, Colorado

However, the financial crisis that hit this nation in the fall of 2008, now known as the Great Recession, destroyed many businesses and people's lifelong savings. While we were in good enough shape to complete the project, the next two years would see advertising fall to record lows, causing several rounds of staff layoffs. Budget cuts were drastic and continuous throughout the corporation, and still we found ourselves just barely treading water. During this period, Dean was elected president of the Colorado Press Association, and the Lehman Communications Print Facility opened its doors for business as we met the scheduled "go live" date of May 19, 2009.

I was always of the opinion the new press would add tremendous value to all the newspaper properties. I also felt it would give us more options for producing our newspaper products and for accommodating a

Opposite, top photo: On the night of May 18, 2009, I started the new press for the first printing of the Loveland Reporter-Herald. *The center photo is a view down the press hall of the manroland Uniset 75, engineered for commercial production. The bottom left photo shows that within minutes the first copies of the paper rolled off the press and down the conveyor belt. At the bottom right, press workers began loading the press with page plates of the first run of the* Loveland Reporter-Herald. *(Photos by Joshua Buck/ Longmont Times-Call and Jill Mott/Longmont Times-Call)*

Dean Lehman in his office at the Times-Call building on Fourth Avenue and Terry Street in Longmont. Dean was president of Lehman Communications from 1987 to 2010, then publisher until he resigned in 2015. Dean was a 34-year-member of the editorial board. (Photo by Lewis Geyer of the Times-Call)

growing variety of commercial print jobs throughout northern Colorado and other western states. I still believe that would have come to pass had we not been so terribly delayed at the outset.

Most people do not wait until they are eighty-five to retire. In earlier years I had asked myself if experience and wisdom could make up for the loss of physical drive and stamina, but I never came up with the answer. Over the years the answer has come to me as a resounding no. With the passage of time, physical drive and stamina diminish while experience and wisdom generally increase. However, life's many variables—including emotional, mental, and physical health and stress levels—can affect one's effectiveness. I missed Ruth's sound business advice and Tom Reeves' ability to see into the future of the newspaper industry. Their counsel was sorely missed during those key pivotal years of 2002 through 2007 when we were doing our analysis and feasibility studies.

Timing is everything. In times of war, battles often have been won or lost due to timing. The same is true for businesses navigating the rough seas of financial planning and logistics. The newspaper business is deadline driven, and events unfold swiftly, requiring daily decision-making. There isn't time for too much pondering. Certainly careful thought and

Ed and Connie Lehman, 2014

consideration go into goal setting and long-term business strategy, but those are generally accomplished well in advance of execution.

It became clear to me with the continually changing and evolving economic conditions that it was time to sell the newspapers. What many people did not realize was this had always been inevitable. *"To everything there is a season"* applies to all of life—businesses as well, quite similar to nature's seasons. The key is to recognize when it is time to begin preparing for the next season.

By late 2009 and early 2010 it was clear we needed to begin making inquiries and preparations for the sale of the newspapers and proceed down this path sooner rather than later.

A last-minute crisis was brewing in Cañon City with the *Daily Record's* classified advertising system, which was running on aging hardware and software. It became imperative we get it stabilized and converted to the same system used by the other papers. The project began in August and was completed by mid-September—not a moment too soon, as it turned out. On the last day of conversion, a backhoe being operated near the building cut a major communications cable, knocking out power for several hours. By the time power was restored the old data server had been damaged beyond repair. We were fortunate that earlier in the week, those directing the conversion operations had printed the remaining accounting reports and all of the classified ads in preparation for input into the new system, thus preserving hard copies of all critical data.

On February 15, 2011, operations and ownership of Lehman Communications Corporation—which included the *Longmont Daily Times-Call, Loveland Daily Reporter-Herald, Cañon City Daily Record,* and the four weeklies, now under the *Colorado Hometown Weekly* umbrella—were turned over to MediaNews Group. Our newspapers became part of the group's subsidiary, Prairie Mountain Publishing, which owned the *Boulder Daily Camera, Colorado Daily,* and ten other newspapers located along the Front Range and in communities in eastern Colorado.

I retired and became editor emeritus, and Dean was named publisher of the Lehman group of newspapers within the Prairie Mountain organization. In June 2015 Dean left Prairie Mountain. However, the story does not end here. Today's sunset is just the start of tomorrow's dawn with new stories to tell.

Chapter Forty

HOLD THE PRESS!

MAKING PREDICTIONS IS A TRICKY BUSINESS because that old nemesis *timing* can change things in ways unimaginable. Many early-day explorers, settlers, and trappers who thought they were headed to certain destinations often found their journey's end in places quite different from where they had imagined. In Grandfather's day exploration opened up westward expansion and brought about the establishment of dynamic cities and communities from the plains of the West to the western side of the Continental Divide all the way to the West Coast.

I find it somewhat ironic that a little over a decade into the twenty-first century many of the same issues and topics are still with us today as they were in Grandfather's time. Certainly the details are different due to our nation's enormous growth and modernization. Still, at the root of all that progress and transformation are many of the same issues—agriculture, water, energy, roads and bridges, wilderness and wildlife protection and management, climate and environmental changes with their attendant effects, communication, economy, real estate development, and sadly, war—to name some of the most critical.

In 2016 we find ourselves in the midst of burgeoning energy exploration and development. Natural gas and oil have moved to the forefront in the energy boom. Gold and silver mines, once so vital to our nation's economy during the nineteenth and twentieth centuries, have moved to a less predominant position in America's economic picture, although they have not entirely disappeared.

Something insufficiently discussed are our nation's nonfuel minerals. Iron, limestone, coal, copper, molybdenum, lead, zinc—to single out just a

Dean Lehman and his wife, Anne, 2013

Lauren Lehman and her husband, John Kivimaki, 2005

few—are crucial to America's energy and economic life. These minerals should be ranked of at least equal importance as natural gas or oil because of their strategic and critical significance to America's national security.

There are few, if any "last frontiers" left, but there are plenty of "continuing frontiers" and "new frontiers." We should be engaged in dynamic discussion surrounding the details of these frontiers because the devil is in the details. Newspapers should be leading the way in these discussions.

What began well over a century ago with Grandfather's story has run through the decades of my life and that of my family. I came to Longmont in 1957 with a dedicated thought. I believed that there could not be a great community without a great newspaper. Acting on this belief, we made every effort possible to publish the best newspapers in our service to the communities of Longmont, Loveland, Cañon City, and the communities surrounding these towns along Colorado's Front Range. Often the work was sweet; just as often it was hard.

Together, my family and I were a force, working in unusual ways to build a better nation and world for the tomorrows ahead. While we may have created the headlines, we were rarely in them. Yet, along our various

Ed and Connie Lehman, 2013

paths, we were dedicated Americans and citizens of our world. In our own ways, we were disciples of the philosophy "To Build a Better World, Start in Your Own Community." It seemed to fit our needs perfectly then, and it has resonated with our readers and endured.

One of the few constants in this world is *change*. As newspaper people, we have been intimately acquainted with *change*. We've watched the communities we've served all grow, mature, and evolve. The newspapers serving each of these communities have transformed too—page by page, subscription by subscription, and employee by employee.

Printing technology has also changed; presses have come and gone. Buildings have been outgrown and replaced. Change for the cities, towns, and their newspapers stretches into the future as unavoidably as the rivers geographically connected to each of them.

In March 2016 Dean attended a joint newspaper publishers' conference with the Inland Press Association and the Southern Newspaper Publishers Association in Austin, Texas. It was reported newspapers' print products are still what pay the bills. Although considerable attention is given to the internet it still is only one aspect of the newspaper industry. It is simply a separate tool of news delivery to a segment of society that is more mobile and prefers to receive their news in an abbreviated way.

One of the biggest challenges for newspapers has been in getting their business models right, not for a lack of readership. People want to read newspapers, but they want genuine information they can trust. News organizations' most valuable resources are their people and the news content. If the news content is honest and trustworthy and presented in an unbiased way advertising and circulation will follow—with hard work, of course. But first, get the news content right.

We all need to embrace and recognize the need for change, not just for the sake of change. The trick is distinguishing between what needs altering and what needs to be maintained. The adage, "If it's not broken, don't fix it," is always worthy of consideration. Walking this thin line between fixing and not fixing can be daunting as well as expensive. Continuous review is required. This is necessary in all areas of life. Don't just trust the changes you've implemented are successful; follow up and verify whether they are or not. They may be successful but there also may be some accompanying unintended consequences, which can often require yet *more* change.

We always felt the role of the newspaper was to be the watchdog keeping people informed about what was going on in their communities, the nation, and the world. Articles explaining what town, city, county, state, and national government officials were doing, or not doing—and providing the *what, when, where, why,* and *how* details—that keep growing populations well informed so they can make necessary decisions. That is how a democracy should function.

In 2016 Longmont is a community of over 100,000 people and encompasses more than 22 square miles. The community has a magnificent view of the Rocky Mountains with more than 300 days of sunshine, and the highest number of people who both live and work in the same city in Boulder County.

I have often said over the years that we had yet to publish our greatest edition. That is still true today. Each dawn is only yesterday's dream, bringing new opportunities.